P9-APF-555

Tasting Italy

Tasting Italy

A Culinary Journey

by
Alice Vollenweider

Translated from the German by
Tim Beech

Armchair Traveller
at the bookHaus

First published in Germany as *Italiens Provinzen und ihre Küche* by Verlag Klaus Wagenbach, 1990

Copyright © 1990 Verlag Klaus Wagenbach, Berlin.

This English translation first published in Great Britain in 2005 by Haus Publishing Limited

This paperback edition published in 2011 by
The Armchair Traveller
at the bookHaus
70 Cadogan Place
London SW1X 9AH
www.thearmchairtraveller.com

The moral rights of the author have been asserted.

A CIP catalogue record for this book is available from the British Library

ISBN 978-1-906598-92-1

Typeset in Garamond by MacGuru Ltd
info@macguru.org.uk
Printed and bound in the UK by CPI Mackays, Chatham ME5 8TD

CONDITIONS OF SALE
All rights reserved. No part of this publication may be reproduced, stored in a retrieval system, or transmitted in any form or by any means, electronic, mechanical, photocopying, recording or otherwise, without the prior permission of the publisher.

This book is sold subject to the condition that it shall not, by way of trade or otherwise, be lent, re-sold, hired out or otherwise circulated without the publisher's prior consent in any form of binding or cover other than that in which it is published and without a similar condition including this condition being imposed on the subsequent purchaser

Contents

Preface,
or the Green Snails of Calabria

*I*t takes a long time to get to know Italy well. You need to travel around, visit cities, and experience everyday life in town and country; go to museums, talk to people; make friends, go to the theatre and the cinema, even read the paper and watch television. Anyone with a special interest in literature and cookery will need to read the authors of the past and the present, and sample dishes in restaurants and in people's homes, as well as studying what is on offer from bookshops and kiosks, markets and super-markets, bakers and fishmongers. Besides all this, it is essential to make comparisons; for example, it is impossible to grasp the true splendour of Carlo Emilio Gadda's recipe for risotto milanese *if you don't know how this risotto is usually cooked, and the discussion about snail-eating in Vittorini's 'Conversation in Sicily' can only be properly understood in the context of the snail-collecting tradition of southern Italian cuisine.*

An intensive involvement with the multifaceted reality of Italy reveals it to be ever richer and ever more complex, so that by the time you finally feel ready to pronounce on it, you discover that during your years of observation things have changed and new developments are taking place. That was my own experience with this book on Italian provincial cookery. It is based on a series of articles written for a magazine over a decade ago which was pub-lished as a book under the title 'Why Parmesan Goes With Almost Every-thing'; it soon went out of print. This new edition contains new chapters and new recipes, and I have largely rewritten the existing text to take account of my subsequent experiences and what has changed since then. As before, the quantities in the recipes are for four people unless otherwise indicated.

Neither geographical nor culinary completeness was my aim in writing this culinary journey through the provinces of Italy. I was less interested in restaurant cuisine than in home cooking, which immediately reveals the style of a region. In Florentine cookery, for example, white beans are at least as important as the enormous bistecca fiorentina, and sardine recipes are a better indicator than fegato alla veneziana of typical Venetian cooking. Italy's history, and the late political unification of kingdoms, duchies and principalities, of maritime and urban republics, each with their own centuries-long history, is one of the reasons why Italian regional cookery has been so well preserved, although the ingredients for any recipe are now available everywhere and, thanks to refrigeration, at any time. The Italians feel that they are Piedmontese, Romans, Tuscans, Lombards or Sicilians; their identity has its roots in their province of origin and not in the unloved state.

This is also reflected in the multiplicity of dialects, which are extraordinarily vigorous in spite of the homogenizing effect of television, school and bureaucracy; this is also demonstrated by the eight hundred page anthology of twentieth-century dialect lyric that was recently published by Einaudi, presenting eighteen authors from Trieste to Lucania.

In the field of gastronomy, it was a century ago that Pellegrino Artusi attempted to compile an anthology of regional specialties; he published his cookery book La scienza in cucina e l'arte di mangiare bene in 1891, and it is still a bestseller. Giorgio Manganelli wrote this about him: 'In the nineteenth century, it was only in the sphere of postage stamps and policemen that Italy was united. That was when Artusi was published. The times entrusted him with a task that he fulfilled with modesty and relentless patience. For more than twenty years, he collected recipes from all the regions of Italy; he juxtaposed the most contradictory exotic rites, the polenta of the Veneto, Sicilian macaroni with sardines and fennel, frogs alla fiorentina, and spinach as it is cooked in Romagna. He entered the mystical space of collective eating as a layman, depicting not the archaic peasant mamma, but the middle-class housewife, a gentle lady of middle years. He uprooted the dishes from *their places of origin, organized them neatly and classified them according to raw materials alone, and in this way he laid the foundations for a national cuisine. Without realizing it, he was a psychologist who influenced the secret pride of the national soul and concentrated it in a single, rich, intense substance; he transferred the local gastronomic traditions into a single codex, a corpus, a catalogue.'*

Despite Manganelli's words of praise for Artusi, the gastronomic unification of Italy has not got very far; the influence of middle-class housewives was restricted to the towns of the industrialized north. The cuisine of the provinces is championed as much as ever, and the authentic, original way to prepare a regional speciality makes for an inexhaustible topic of conversation in almost every setting, at home and in restaurants, on the piazza and in the bar. Of course, the food industry and kitchen and refrigeration technology have gained a foothold in Italian cuisine too, and influenced cooking and eating habits. Today a herb sauce like pesto genovese *will be made in a blender, even though it does taste that bit better when it is crushed in a mortar. Grated cheese in a bag, three-minute polenta and many tinned and deep-frozen foods are a regular part of daily life. In the self-service section of the dining car between Rome and Milan, pasta or meat and vegetables can be bought in ice-cold plastic containers that you heat up in a microwave after paying for them. The food industry even caters for the popularity of regional cookery: they offer the Piedmontese* fonduta, *made from melted cheese, in tins, and sell the buckwheat pasta of the Valtellina,* pizzocheri, *in boxes.*

Nonetheless, in Italy one eats better than one does on average in Europe. This is true both of restaurants and home cooking, quite simply because flavour and delight in good food are part of good living. People are prepared to pay for this enjoyment; they don't buy their pasta from the supermarket, but in a special shop where ravioli, tortellini and pasta are freshly prepared every day, and they get their peas shelled by the grocer, though of course they cost more like that than if they were bought frozen. The Italian food industry does include small firms that take an interest in quality and whose goods bear comparison with home-made produce. One example is the firm of Fini, which owns the best restaurant and the most comfortable hotel in Modena and runs three motorway service stations and a food factory on the outskirts of the city, where the famous Fini products are made: tortellini and tortelloni, mortadella and zampone, balsamic vinegar and nocino, the walnut liqueur of Emilia. These are all products that the traveller in Italy likes to think he can expect to be served home made. The kitchen of the Ristorante Fini, awarded two stars in the Guide Michelin, uses the firm's own products, that is vacuum-packed tortellini and sausages. There are other trends, too, that presage a gastronomic future that is not altogether bleak. In Italy too, there is a growing interest in healthy eating and whole foods, and people perceive this not as a weird alternative, but as a return to mother's or grandmother's cooking; here, the humble pulses such as beans, broad beans, chickpeas and lentils never left the menu, and the same is true of old types of grain like buckwheat or spelt, which in many provinces were handed down from an agrarian past that lies no more than forty years back.

The intensity with which the old peasant world continues to affect the technologised present, above all in southern Italy, is made apparent in the books of Tommaso Di Ciaula, the son of peasants and a worker; they portray the new forms of life of the society of factories and mass consumption with aggressive humour. In his first book The Factory Ape and the Trees he wrote: "You used to be able to live off festivals. If you went to all the festivals, you could just eat for nothing. When the cuttlefish festival was on in Mola di Bari, you would just go to Mola to eat cuttlefish. Another festival was the 'calzoni' one, pizza dough filled with onions; that was in Acquaviva delle Fonti. In Mariotto there was the grape festival, and in San Michele the festival of the 'zampine', fried pigs' trotters." The survival of these eating festivals in southern Italy as a living tradition is demonstrated by the curious story of the snail festival of Santa Maria di Catanzaro, told to me by a friend from Catanzaro. It was about ten years ago that people in Santa Maria, a small town of fifteen thousand inhabitants, began to breed the popular Calabrian snails of the area. These are little snails with stripy green shells; they are sold in the markets as vermiture or dormiture, and they are in such high demand that a kilo of snails costs more than a kilo of veal. The snails are bred with much care and expertise in courtyards and gardens, and this has gradually turned into a lucrative hobby for office and factory workers, teachers and craftsmen. The obvious next step was the proclamation in 1989 of a snail festival, a sagra della vermitura. A wood carver had carved a giant snail out of an olive trunk for the occasion; it was carried through the streets at the head of the festival procession to the sound of band music. There was then a meal on the piazza, consisting of snail stew, bread and wine. But the snail enthusiasts were not expecting that their over-strict priest would publicly condemn the pagan procession; this led to outraged disputes in the local paper, and eventually to a split among the population of the town between the opponents and the advocates of the snails.

This quarrel did no harm to the gastronomical cause; on the contrary, the search is now under way for districts in Tuscany or Piedmont with which to establish a friendship pact under the banner of the snail. The assumption, which is surely correct, is that there are always going to be plenty of demanding eaters in Italy who will band together just as enthusiastically to defend their passion when it is under threat as they do to indulge it.

Como,
or why sage goes with fish

While Sergio was still living in Como, that was where I generally used to break my journey to Florence, Rome or Naples. Como is a good way to get into the mood of Italy: the walled heart of the town goes back to Roman times, a rectangle five hundred and fifty metres by four hundred in which there are elegant residential streets, fine *palazzi* and a cathedral which abuts the town hall, an ensemble which forms one of the most beautiful architectural complexes in Lombardy. And from the quay, the shimmering water of the lake can be seen; on its banks, the old villa gardens ascend the steep slope with limes, rhododendrons, magnolias and gardenias. The Italians know Lake Como from their schooldays, when they will have had to read Alessandro Manzoni's *I promessi sposi* ('The Betrothed'). This most famous of all Italian novels opens with a splendidly exact, indeed almost pedantic description of the landscape surrounding the lake; the first sentence runs: "The southern arm of lake Como which lies between two unbroken chains of mountains that in their advance and retreat form numerous promontories and bays at the end quite suddenly becomes very narrow, taking on the form and current of a river between the foothills to the right and a broad bank on the left."

I can still remember my first evening in Como well. It was a fine mild March day. Sergio picked me up from the station, and over a Campari in the "Lili Bar", he told me his wife was covering for a sick colleague at the paper and wouldn't be home till around eleven. But this did not prevent him from inviting me to have dinner with him, though of course Sergio can't cook. He just served me Linetta's specialities: marinated fish as a starter, followed by minestrone with grated Parmesan, bread and red wine. We finished with *formaggini*, little round alpine cheeses. But the gourmets of Lombardy and Ticino do not eat their *formaggini* fresh and bland like the clueless tourists from the north; they put them on a wooden board to ripen in a cool place until they have acquired a rind and a slightly runny, aromatic consistency. Then they are ready to receive a grating of pepper from the mill and a gentle sprinkling of olive oil. That was the evening when I realized the true meaning of hospitality. It has nothing to do with the ceremony of invitation and reciprocation, as is our habit. Rather, it is a way of life based on living companionably with one's fellow human beings and being prepared to share food and drink with them.

Even the marinated fish – known around the Lombard lakes as *pesce in carpione* – is a hospitable dish that is never prepared for a single occasion. They are made for keeping, and the recipe comes from a time when the deep freeze had not yet been invented. Instead, the fried fish were bottled in a vinegar marinade, allowing them to be kept in the cellar for at least two weeks. Linetta subsequently entrusted me with her recipe.

Pesce in carpione
Marinated fish
1 kg whitefish, trout, or any white fish
flour, peanut oil
For the marinade:
1 onion, 2 carrots, 1 stick of celery
500 ml wine vinegar
500 ml white wine
salt, pepper and red wine vinegar to taste

½ teaspoon sugar
thyme, marjoram
1 bay leaf
2 sage leaves
1 bunch of parsley

Turn the fish in the flour. After shaking the flour off well, fry them in the hot oil till they are golden yellow and lay them on kitchen paper to absorb surplus oil.

For the marinade, slice the onion, carrots and celery finely and melt them gently in the oil the fish were fried in, covered. Sprinkle with ½ tablespoon flour and continue cooking; then add the red wine vinegar and the white wine. Season with salt, pepper and sugar, with thyme, marjoram, bay, sage and the finely-chopped parsley. Bring the marinade to a boil and leave to simmer on low heat for half an hour, till the vegetables are soft. Once the marinade has cooled, pour over the fish, which have previously been arranged next to each other in a flat dish. They must be completely covered by the liquid. Cover the dish with tin foil and put it somewhere cool for a day. These marinated fish can be kept for 10–14 days without any problem; they get increasingly soft and aromatic. They may be served as a starter or as a main course. Fillets may be used instead of whole fish.

The true nature of hospitality is not the only thing I learned from Linetta. In her bright, clean kitchen with its big marble table I also worked out that the key to the art of cooking is not primarily imagination, but above all experience, moderation and accuracy. For her, each culinary herb has its own clearly delimited sphere, and she finds it puzzling that there are supposedly housewives north of the Alps who use dried mixed herbs. She only ever uses fresh herbs, and when basil, tarragon and dill wilt in the autumn, then she just limits herself to sage, rosemary and oregano, which grow all year round in her little herb garden. It is probably thanks to this limitation that she noticed how well the bitter taste of sage goes with the fish from Lake Como. I will never forget her *lavarelli alla salvia*, a kind of whitefish that she braises in a heatproof dish in the oven. Making them is child's play; sprinkle them with salt, pour melted butter over them, add two sage leaves, and baste them a few times with their juices while they cook for fifteen minutes.

Linetta's minestrone, too, is as it were a classic dish, but the ingredients for it can be found throughout the year in the garden. Summer vegetables such as peas, cucumbers, or aubergines, let alone peppers, would be out of place.

Minestrone
Vegetable soup

Ingredients for four (but it is worth making double):
50 g diced bacon
2–3 sage leaves
2–3 cloves of garlic
30 g butter
1 small head Savoy cabbage
1–2 leeks
2–3 carrots
1 stick of celery
1 bunch of parsley
2–3 potatoes
250 g borlotti beans
100 g parmesan
1 litre water and a stock cube or
2 litres meat stock
salt and pepper

Soak the speckled little borlotti beans overnight in cold water. Drain, cover the beans with fresh cold water and boil for 1½–2 hours till tender. This is a precautionary measure, as certain chemical processes may prevent the beans from cooking properly together with the other vegetables. If freshly picked beans are available in late summer, they should be mixed directly with the other vegetables, that have been cleaned, washed and chopped as finely as possible. Then melt the butter – preferably in a heavy-bottomed pot – and fry the bacon till it is transparent. Add the vegetables and herbs (but not the potatoes) and continue cooking till their liquid covers the base of the pan. Add the hot stock (or water with stock cube), season, bring to the boil and finally add the peeled and very finely cut up potatoes; during the cooking they will disintegrate and thicken the liquid. Cook on a low heat for 1½ hours. Then add the borlotti beans and simmer for a further 30 minutes. If the minestrone is not thick enough, raise the heat and remove the lid for the last few minutes.

An important variant of minestrone is *busecca*, the tripe soup that is so popular both around the Lombard lakes and in the valleys of Ticino. It is made in just the same way as minestrone, except that after 1½ hours, a pound of finely chopped tripe is added together with the borlotti beans before the final half an hour of cooking.

One simple and delicious desert I have eaten both in Como and in Ticino is called *busecchina*, 'little tripe soup', probably because the light beige of the dried chestnuts it is made from resembles the colour of tripe.

This country dish, for which I would gladly give up all the oversweet desserts of the world, contains the secret of all good cookery: a pure, authentic natural product like the chestnut, carefully cooked at the right moment.

Busecchina
Chestnut dessert

500 g dried chestnuts
water
1 glass white wine
200 ml cream

Soak the chestnuts overnight in lukewarm water. Drain, and clean off the remaining brown skins with a hard brush. Wash the chestnuts, cover with cold water, add the white wine and cook on very low heat till soft. This will take 1½–2 hours. If the cooking liquid reduces too quickly, add another cup or two of hot water. Finally the chestnuts will have soaked up almost all the liquid, and the bottom of the pot will be covered by a pink sauce with a sweet and penetrating aroma. Serve the chestnuts on little plates or in glass bowls with a little of the sauce, and pour cream over them.

Today Sergio and Linetta live in Milan, but Como has remained an important landmark for me. One reason for this is that it is in Como that the concerts of the 'autunno musicale' are held, against the splendid classicising backdrop of the Villa Olmi; another is that the Seteria Martinetti is in Como. This is where boutiquiers and seamstresses from half Lombardy buy their stock; in the back is a fabric paradise, with thousands of rolls of silk lying on the shelves, where ultra-fine linens await their transformation into tailored shirts. Sometimes I also look in at Gerosa, the all-modern light shop not far from the entrance to the *città murata*; every other client is a German-speaker who has come from Ticino. Another good reason to go to Como is that you can eat better there than is now possible in Ticino, overrun as it is by tourists. One excellent place is the 'Trattoria delle Catene', which serves authentic local dishes such as polenta with stewed snails or risotto with borlotti beans. This is also where I first ate *Crema del Lario*, a bold and brilliant combination of whipped cream and lemon.

Crema del Lario
Whipped lemon cream

250 ml cream
50 g sugar
½ lemon
2 small glasses of grappa

Beat the cream till stiff and mix carefully with the sugar and grated lemon rind. Stir constantly while adding the lemon juice; the whipped cream will absorb the sour liquid without clotting. Finally, add the grappa, place the cream in glass bowls and keep them in the fridge till they are served.

Piedmont,
or a taste of France

Long before I first went to Piedmont, I had many varied and vivid notions about this province and its capital Turin; these derived above all, of course, from the work of Cesare Pavese, in which the hilly landscape of Monferrato, with its vineyards, forests and villages, is present as a mythical land of lost childhood. I also knew it from Natalia Ginzburg's *Family Encyclopedia*, which tells the story of her family in direct unfictionalised form, as well as sketching the history of Turin in the thirties and forties, with all its culture and its political courage. Finally, I knew it from the detective novels of Fruttero and Lucentini, who portray with accomplished charm the labyrinth of Turin society between industry, the *demi-monde* and the mafia underworld.

The famous Piedmontese cuisine, which combines French subtlety with natural Italian ingredients, was also not unknown to me. After all, the white truffles of Alba are exported the world over. Consuming them demonstratively is not necessarily a measure of gastronomic sensibility, and Luigi Malerba once told me the way to eat truffles politely even with a heavy cold – you have to make the right grimaces at the right moment, so as to document the unmatchable splendour of the flavour you have supposedly just enjoyed.

I even got to know the classic *bagna cauda* (hot sauce), the greatgrandmother of all fondues, outside Piedmont – in Naples with homesick exiles from Turin. This sauce, made from oil, butter, garlic and anchovies, is stirred in an earthenware pot and kept warm at the table. Rather than dipping meat or bread cubes in it, you dip raw vegetables, which is healthier and more varied. Cardoons are the classic vegetable accompaniment, the blanched stems of a variety of thistle (French *cardons*, Italian *cardi*); celery tastes very good too, as do fennel, peppers, cauliflower and artichokes.

It was in 1966 that I first went to Turin, for the opening night of Natalia Ginzburg's comedy *Ti ho sposato per allegria* in the Teatro Carignano. I immediately felt at home in this town; long winding residential streets lead from the station to the centre, where the great piazzas with their baroque palaces, churches and monuments open up. It's hardly surprising that Giorgio De Chirico's *pittura metafisica* was inspired by Turin. He saw the town for the first time in 1911, and wrote: 'The magic of Turin is still further accentuated by the perpendicular, geometrical layout of the streets and squares and by the arcades, under which you can stroll in all weathers. These promenades make the town look as though it had been constructed for philosophical conversations, gatherings and meditation. In Turin, everything is appearance. On reaching a square, you find yourself facing a man of stone who stares at you as only statues can. The horizon is sometimes blocked by a wall behind which the whistling of locomotives or the noise of an arriving train may be heard. The geometrical precision of the squares reveals the totality of longing for the infinite.'

It was a rainy day in May, and I enjoyed walking under the arcades of the town centre without an umbrella and looking at patriarchally elegant establishments with gilded shop signs; inside, fashionable clothes, fine materials and gastronomic delicacies were tastefully arranged. After the premiere, which received hearty applause from an audience of friends and acquaintances, we went to have dinner in a restaurant whose name I have now forgotten. But I can still remember the menu: there were *gnocchi à la piémontaise*, in a tomato sauce, and *vitello tonnato*, both of the highest quality, accompanied by a young Barbera with a rich bouquet. Marisa later gave me the recipe for the gnocchi.

Gnocchi di patate alla piemontese
Piedmontese potato gnocchi

1 kg potatoes
200 g wheat flour
2 eggs
salt

Cook the potatoes in their skins, peel them while still warm and put them through a sieve. Then allow them to cool a little; mix them with the beaten eggs, the flour and a little salt, and knead this dough until it no longer sticks to the hands. With floured hands, roll out finger-thick rolls and cut these into 2 cm lengths. Lay these pieces of dough one by one on a fork held in the left hand. Press down on the dough with the thumb of the right hand, so that it curls up a little, producing the typical shell shape of the gnocchi, marked by the tines of the fork. Cook them for just a few minutes in well-salted water, lifting them out with a slotted spoon as soon as they come up to the surface. Drain well and place in a warmed dish.

These gnocchi taste best when you pour melted butter over them; you can add a sage leaf to the butter while it is warming. Sprinkle generously with grated Parmesan. They may also be served with tomato or meat sauce.

Veal in tuna sauce (*vitello tonnato*) is one of the subtlest and best Italian meat dishes. It was Marisa who told me that it is a speciality of Piedmont; she explained to me that salt fish *conserves*, such as tuna or sardines in oil or salt, and of course salt cod (*baccalà*) are typical of her native province, which nowhere reaches the sea.

Vitello tonnato
Veal in tuna sauce

Ingredients for 6:
1 kg veal (shoulder)
1 carrot
1 onion (stuck with 2 cloves and a bay leaf)
300 g tuna
2 anchovy fillets
200 ml olive oil
yolks of 2 eggs
1 tablespoon capers
salt

Cook the meat with the onion and the carrot in salted water on a very low heat until it is done; this should take about an hour and a half, then leave it to cool in its liquid. Purée the drained tuna, the anchovies and 100 ml of the veal stock to make a thick sauce; add the finely-chopped capers to it. Make a mayonnaise from the eggs and olive oil; season with lemon juice and salt before adding to the tuna sauce. If necessary, thin the sauce again with some of the cooking liquid. Now remove the cold meat from its juice and slice it. Place the slices in the original shape of the joint and place in a deep bowl, not too large. Pour the sauce over the meat and allow the flavour to develop for a few hours, or even overnight in the fridge. To serve, arrange the slices in a tile pattern on a flat surface, stir the sauce well and pour it over the meat. Decorate the platter with quartered eggs, salted cucumbers or olives.

NB It is also possible to coat chicken breasts with a tuna

*mayonnaise; whitefish or trout fillets go excellently with this
sauce too.*

The next day I had a lunch appointment in the 'Ristorante del Cambio'
with a friend from the publisher Einaudi. Entering this elegant establishment is like diving into the nineteenth century: endless high ceilings,
crystal chandeliers, red plush, mirrors and frescoes create an atmosphere
of luxury, and the first Kings of Italy look down from the walls in splendid
frames. You get the feeling that Cavour was once a regular here. French
and Piedmontese specialities both figure on the menu. The warm starters were of exceptional quality: tiny little portions of delicately spiced
mussels, fish, crab, sweetbreads, delicate vegetables and mushrooms.

In spite of the Cambio menu's enticing range of traditional specialities
from the butter and cream-rich Piedmontese cuisine – from *salsa finan-
ziera*, which includes cocks' combs and veal marrow, to the exquisite
vegetables in cream or béchamel sauce – we went straight from starter
to dessert, and I made the acquaintance of *panna cotta* (cooked cream),
a mound of cream stiffened with gelatine that was served with fresh wild
strawberries and had a fine flavour. I acquired the recipe years later from
Christoph and Rosanna, who had eaten the *panna cotta* in a restaurant in
the Ligurian town of Bonassola. They were not let into the secret of how
it is made, and ever since, Christoph has been experimenting successfully
with this dessert. His *panna cotta* is finished off with caramelised sugar,
like crême brulée.

Panna cotta
Boiled cream

Ingredients for 8:
1 litre cream

2 tablespoons icing sugar
3 vanilla pods
5 sheets gelatine
80 g sugar
amaretto liqueur

Dissolve the gelatine in lukewarm water. Bring the cream to the boil with the icing sugar and the inside of the vanilla pods; remove the pan from the heat, allow the cream to cool slightly and amalgamate it with the gelatine, stirring vigorously. Then caramelize the sugar in a pan and use it to coat individual moulds, which should then be filled with the cream. To allow the caramel to be properly absorbed, put the moulds in the fridge for half a day. To serve, dip the moulds briefly in hot water and invert them over a plate with a teaspoon of amaretto on it. When panna cotta is served with fresh berries, it should be made without caramel.

I got to know the Piedmont countryside a few years later when Lorenzo and I travelled from Laigueglia on the Riviera via Turin, the Val d'Aosta and the Great St Bernard Pass back to Switzerland. Our first port of call was Alba, the capital of Langhe, home of the great red wines of Piedmont and of the white truffle. It was in September, shortly before the vintage; the uniform ranges of hills with their terraced vineyards, as far as the eye could see, interrupted only here and there by hazelnut bushes, yellow strips of sand and isolated farmsteads or half-ruined towers, were reminiscent of Pavese: 'A vineyard that climbs up a hillside till it cuts into the sky is a familiar sight; yet the simple deep rows appear like curtains in front of a magical gate. Beneath the vines the red earth has been broken, the leaves hide treasures, and beyond them lies the sky. It is a sky ever softer, ever riper, with no trace of the September clouds, its own treasures and vines. All this is familiar and yet distant; in short, it belongs to childhood, but each time it is disturbing, as if it were a whole world.'

Another great Piedmontese writer also comes from this area: Beppe Fenoglio, in whose gloomy and dramatic resistance novels the hills of the Langhe almost always appear shrouded in rain, fog or snow, lived from 1922 to 1963 in Alba, where he was manager of a great wine producing firm. We saw the house where he was born, on the Piazza Rossetti next to the gothic cathedral.

Alba is a gourmet's town, and it is almost impossible to find a bad restaurant there. That evening we went to an unpretentious trattoria near the station that had a lot of custom – in Italy, this is almost always a good sign. We ordered a *bollito misto*, and were impressed by its quality and variety. Not only was there juicy boiled beef, veal, tongue and chicken, but also head of veal and *cotechino*, a spicy pork sausage. The dish was accompanied by bread, *salsa verde*, gherkins and pickled onions. Today I still make my *salsa verde* according to the recipe the landlord gave me when I asked him.

Salsa verde
Green sauce

1 bunch of parsley
1 clove of garlic
2 anchovy fillets or some anchovy paste
salt and pepper
1 tablespoon wine vinegar
3 tablespoons olive oil
2–3 tablespoons hot stock
breadcrumbs

Chop the parsley, garlic and anchovies very finely and mix in the wine vinegar and the breadcrumbs. Gradually stir in the

oil; season with salt and freshly-milled pepper. Leave the sauce
to develop flavour for half an hour, thinning it somewhat with
hot stock before serving.

The tiny pickled onions tasted far more aromatic and appealing than north of the Alps. This is due both to the higher quality of Italian onions and to the fact that they are pickled in mild wine vinegar, which not only gives them their good flavour, but makes them a fine red colour too.

Cipolline sott'aceto
Pickled onions

1 kg pickling onions or shallots
10 g salt
1 litre good red wine vinegar
20 peppercorns
4 bay leaves

Bring the vinegar to the boil with the other ingredients and boil
the peeled onions in it in batches for 1–2 minutes. Then remove
them and place in little jars or in an earthenware pot. Once the
vinegar is cold, pour it over them, including the peppercorns
and bay leaves. The onions must be covered by the vinegar. After
two to three days, pour the vinegar off again, boil it up and pour
it back once it has cooled. Then cover the jars or pot and keep in
a cool place.

Saracen's wheat and wine
from the Valtellina

My first acquaintance with the cooking of the Valtellina was made in a Zurich restaurant, the St. Jakob on the Stauffacher. The proprietor, Karl Bienz, is married to a woman from the Valtellina; she taught him how to make *pizzocheri*. On his wedding day he ate six platefuls of this nutritious Valtellina speciality, and since then he has also cooked *pizzocheri* for people from both Zurich and the Valtellina in his restaurant. They do not appear on the menu, though; you have to order them in advance, for a minimum of five people, otherwise it is not worth the chef's while to make them. *Pizzocheri* are a meat-free dish that combines in an imaginative and tasty way all the natural produce that a poor mountain valley offers its inhabitants: butter, cheese, garlic, potatoes, Savoy cabbage and home-made buckwheat pasta.

Buckwheat is one of the oldest cultivated plants, so easy to please that it will grow on poor sandy soils and in mountainous situations; it can thrive anywhere from the Russian steppes to the Alpine valleys of Italy. Its three-cornered, nut-like grains resemble beech mast. It was rediscovered in the alternative cooking of the seventies. Like barley, oats, millet and rye, it is one of the wholesome and tasty wholemeal grains; for this reason it contains far more minerals and vitamin B than normal wheat flour. In the Middle Ages it was cultivated throughout Europe wherever the climate was too harsh for wheat. In Italy it is called *grano saraceno*, in France *blé sarrasin*, or Saracen's wheat; north of the Alps it was named 'heathen corn'.

This name may have referred to the origin of the grain in Arab lands, or to its dark colour, for in the Middle Ages all Muslims of the Mediterranean area were termed Saracens. Today buckwheat is only cultivated in borderlands, the Valtellina, the Steiermark, in former Yugoslavia and in parts of Russia, where it is used to make the famous blinis, which are distantly related to the *crêpes de sarrasin* of Brittany. As buckwheat does not contain gluten, it must be combined with other flours or with eggs to make the dough cohere.

My *pizzocheri* recipe for ten comes from the restaurant 'St Jakob'. It uses half buckwheat and half wheat flour, but in the Valtellina the flours are combined at a ratio of two to one.

Pizzocheri
Buckwheat pasta

Ingredients for 10:
750 g buckwheat flour
750 g wheat flour
1 medium Savoy cabbage
4 potatoes
300 g butter
5 cloves of garlic
300 g grated Parmesan

Stir the two flours together with lukewarm water to make a firm pasta dough; roll it out, not too thin, and cut into 5 cm by 1 cm strips. Then bring a large pan of salt water to the boil and add the cabbage, cut into strips. When it is half done, add the cubed potatoes and the pasta; it should be done in about twenty minutes. Meanwhile, melt the butter, gently fry the pressed

*garlic in it, and then sieve the golden-brown garlic butter and
keep warm. Serve by lifting pasta, cabbage and potatoes out of
the water with a slotted spoon and placing it in layers on a dish.
Each layer should be given a generous sprinkling of Parmesan
and drenched in garlic butter. Herr Bienz recommends mixing
the Parmesan with a little grated Emmental; this creates a fine
flavour as well as the odd thread of cheese, which goes well with
this dish. As I found out later, in the Valtellina they use little
slices of hard local cheese instead of grated Parmesan. Green
beans or Swiss chard stems or leaves may be used instead of the
Savoy cabbage, and the garlic butter can be replaced with
onions gently fried in butter.*

Pizzocheri are so well-known in Lombardy that the food industry has
latched on to them; in a pasta factory in Morbeno in the Valtellina they
are produced by machine and packed by the pound. These easy *pizzocheri*,
which can also be bought in Milan and Zurich supermarkets, are supposedly so popular that the Valtellina's buckwheat crop is no longer sufficient
for their manufacture, with the result that buckwheat is imported from
the Soviet Union and only the milling now takes place in Valtellina mills.

It was thanks to Lorenzo that I was introduced to eating *pizzocheri*;
he had connections among the Valtellina community in Zurich, because
his father comes from the Valtellina valley. It was with him that I set off
for a look at the Valtellina one fine autumn day. The journey through the
Hinterrhein valley and then along the winding old Splügen pass road
to Chiavenna was beautiful and varied, but I found the Valtellina itself
rather disappointing, with its long flat valley; the fields and the buildings
along the main road created a rather monotonous effect in the translucent
autumn light. The landscape does become more attractive as you approach
Sondrio, with its steep, closely ranged vineyards clinging to the precipices
on the right-hand side of the valley. The four cultivation areas, after which
the classic Valtellina wines are also named, are Sassella, Grumello, Inferno
and Valgella; they are spread out along the hillsides above the valley floor

for seventy kilometres from Castione to Teglio. Lorenzo told me how he met an old wine grower on a previous visit to Montagna, his father's village; this man invited him into his cellar, where they tried wines of different vintages with a *boccale*, an earthenware jug holding a litre. They also had Valtellina rye bread and salami. This good wine just gave Lorenzo a pleasant feeling of euphoria, with no trace of a hangover.

In Sondrio we took possession of a room in an old hotel on the Piazza Garibaldi before going for a walk in the sleepy, peaceful provincial capital. We struck up a conversation with some locals in a bar, and when we asked them to recommend a good restaurant, a long, thoughtful discussion ensued that only came to an end when all of our new acquaintances had agreed on one establishment. Someone offered to drive us there in his car.

The landlord, himself a wine grower, runs his restaurant as a family business with a degree of care and concern for quality rare even in Italy. In France, he would have got at least one star from the *Guide Michelin*. As an antipasto he recommended the *bresàola*, the local name for wind-dried beef. Unlike *Bündner Fleisch* (a Swiss equivalent), instead of being just speared off the plate, it is transformed into a delicacy by being thinly coated in a sauce made of olive oil, a few drops of lemon juice and freshly grated black pepper. The fame of the raw meat salad from Piedmont, internationally known under the name *carpaccio*, derives from the same recipe. Many locals season this marinade with thyme, marjoram and oregano as well as pepper.

The next course was a simple and harmonious combination of the best the Valtellina streams and valleys have to offer:

Trotelle con funghi porcini
Trout fillets with ceps
8 small or 4 large trout fillets

400 g fresh (or frozen) ceps
50 g butter
2 tablespoons oil
white wine
salt and pepper
thyme
1–2 cloves of garlic
1 bunch of parsley

*Marinate the trout fillets for one hour in white wine seasoned
with salt, pepper and thyme. Slice the mushrooms, heat oil in a
pan, fry gently for five minutes with the finely-chopped garlic,
sprinkle with the chopped parsley and allow to simmer a few
minutes longer. Then heat the butter in another pan and fry
the trout fillets slowly and carefully on a low heat; finally, add
the wine from the marinade and reduce slightly at a higher
temperature. Serve the trout on a platter covered with ceps; you
may wish to sprinkle some melted butter over them.*

Butter plays an important role in the cooking of the Valtellina. Our host
made it clear that if possible, he does not cook with the bland butter from
the dairy, but uses tasty alpine butter from private producers. Cream, too,
is found in this cholesterol-rich cuisine. On feast days, polenta used to be
cooked in cream instead of water, and meat sauces too are often finished
off with cream.

For the main course, we ordered the chamois casserole; its unique
flavour is due to the cocoa that is added at the end of cooking, together
with some cream and a shot of grappa.

Salmì di camoscio
Chamois casserole

Ingredients for six:
2 kg chamois pieces for stewing
50 g diced bacon
20 g cocoa
150 g carrots
150 g onions
150 g celeriac
1 clove of garlic
2 juniper berries
2 cloves
1 bay leaf
1 piece cinnamon
peppercorns
2 tablespoons flour
100 ml cream
a bottle of good Valtellina wine
1 small glass grappa
oil and salt

Wash and peel the vegetables. Slice the carrots, cut the onions in rings and cube the celeriac, and place in a narrow dish with high sides. Pour in the wine, add the spices (garlic, juniper, cloves, bay, cinnamon, peppercorns) and place the meat in this marinade, which should cover it completely.

After 24 hours, pour off the marinade. Reserve. Fry the bacon in hot oil till transparent, add the meat and fry on high heat until it begins to brown. Then sprinkle with flour and continue

frying until the flour colours. Add the wine from the marinade,
season and leave to simmer on low heat for no more than two
hours. Now add the cocoa, dissolved in cream. Bring briefly to
the boil, pour over the grappa and remove from the heat.

With the chamois casserole we had *polenta negra*, the flavourful dark Valtellina polenta made of three parts buckwheat to one part corn.

With our espresso the owner brought two wonderfully scented, crumbly corn cakes as an *omaggio della casa*; his wife bakes them fresh every day. She wrote down her simple recipe for me.

Torta di granoturco
Corn cake

250 g fine corn meal
250 g flour
250 g butter
250 g sugar
4 eggs
10 g baking powder
salt
small glass grappa

Melt the butter over water, stir it together with the two flours,
and add the sugar, the yolks of the eggs, the salt, the baking
powder and the grappa. Beat the whites till stiff and fold into
the mixture. Place in a buttered springform dusted with corn
meal, and bake the cake for 40 minutes in a medium oven.

Since then, I have often baked this cake. It also goes well with a glass of dessert wine or with the grappa-flavoured blueberries that I tried for the first time on that memorable evening in Sondrio. They are apparently simple to make. Combine 1 kg blueberries with 300 g sugar, leave in an uncovered jar in the sun for a week, fill up with grappa, put the lid on and keep in the cellar for a few weeks.

Risotto alla Milanese

At first sight, Milan is neither beautiful nor inviting. The Italians say the reason the Milanese are so famously hard-working is that they have nothing to seduce them into inactivity: no seaside, no lake, no mountains, not so much as a hill. Just bad weather. It really is true that in winter the city is swathed for days or even weeks in cold, damp fog, and in the summer the air in the streets of the Lombard metropolis is often unbearably close. What is more, Milan has too many factories, too much concrete, too many multi-storey car parks and supermarkets. Even the air is worse than in other big European cities. And still, each time I walk out onto the broad square in front of the train station and see before me the bold and elegant silhouette of the skyscraper built by the architects Ponti and Nervi for the firm of Pirelli, I feel glad to be there.

I'm not exactly sure what it is about Milan that makes me feel so comfortable; it has something to do with the buzz in the city centre, where precious witnesses of the past – Roman columns and baroque portals, Romanesque basilicas and neoclassical palaces – stand surrounded by indifferent or ugly modern buildings in the midst of the flow of traffic, only noticed by curious pedestrians. Pedestrians are few and far between in this busy, industrious city, but it is Milan more than any other Italian town that entices me to walk in it, because, in the absence of the travel-brochure prettiness – sometimes almost too lovely – of other Italian towns, you feel like discovering its unassuming beauties for yourself.

What's more, in the centre of Milan are the best bars in the whole of

Italy. They are sparklingly clean, each with its own character, and they make the heart of Milan feel like one huge welcoming salon where you can always find somewhere to have a quick drink or a bite to eat, or a chat with someone. These bars are emblematic of the ease of social contact, as is shown by their glass walls, which abolish the distinction between inside and outside, and their almost constantly open doors. The bar is a kind of continuation of the street; there is no compulsion to have anything, and you can just pop in to say hello to someone, buy cigarettes or make a phone call. It has something of the quality of a small stage, where the customers are the actors. You stand still and move about, go and pay at the till, and you can see your reflection in all the mirrors.

There is no lack of good restaurants in Milan either. There is one foolproof way to test the mettle of an unknown establishment. Order *risotto alla milanese*, and its quality will reflect the quality of the cooking in general. You can tell a good risotto just by looking at it: it should be golden yellow, shiny and thick, but each grain of rice should still be separate, and cooked *al dente*. Pulling this feat off calls for twenty minutes' intense concentration at the stove.

Twenty years ago, the rice for risotto could either be Vialone or Arborio; now the cooks of northern Italy all agree that Carnaroli rice is the best. It produces a creamy risotto like Vialone, but is less inclined to burn, and remains chewy for up to ten minutes past the proper cooking time. It is more expensive than the other kinds, though, and not widely known outside Italy.

Risotto alla milanese

400 g Vialone or Carnaroli rice
1 onion
80 g butter

50 g beef marrow
(2–3 big marrow bones)
1 litre meat stock
pinch saffron
50 g grated Parmesan

Melt the butter with the marrow and stew the finely-chopped onion in it. Add the rice and fry it well. Add a little boiling stock, stir with a wooden spoon and wait till the liquid has been fully absorbed. Continue gradually adding the rest of the stock in this way, ensuring that the risotto is boiling on high heat from start to finish; this means it must be stirred constantly to prevent it burning. After a quarter of an hour, add the saffron, taking care during the last five minutes' cooking time not to miss the transition of the rice from hard to chewy. To this end it is advisable to add the liquid in very small quantities at this stage and keep trying a forkful of rice. Remove the risotto from the heat and mix in half of the grated Parmesan. The rest of the cheese is served separately at table.

Risotto alla milanese, this simple and aristocratic Milanese speciality, is held in esteem by rich and poor throughout northern Italy, just like onion soup in Paris or pizza in Naples, though it should be said that neither of these two solid and wholesome dishes possesses the aroma or the easy digestibility of a true Milanese risotto. Risotto may be served as a starter or as a main course, and it rounds off a night of celebration, dancing and drinking with more ceremony than a hearty soup or grilled sausages and beer. What is more, its imperishable ingredients can always be kept on hand. Finally, the rice, which is far more highly valued throughout Lombardy than pasta, is a local product of nature. More rice is harvested in the Po area than all the inhabitants of Milan and of Italy itself could consume between them.

Risotto is such a perfect dish that it really ought to be enjoyed without any accompaniment apart from a good glass of red wine, but there is one great exception to this rule. *Ossobuco*, braised shin of veal, goes brilliantly with risotto, and in Milan these two dishes are always served together. There are those who object that it's just typical of the Milanese to eat the first and second courses of a meal from the same plate, so they can get back to work quicker afterwards.

Ossobuco alla milanese
Stewed shin of veal

4 veal shins, sawn into slices
1 medium onion
1 bunch of parsley
1 carrot
a few sage leaves
50 g butter
2 tablespoons tomato purée
500–750 ml meat stock

Chop the vegetables extremely finely; they should no longer be visible after 2½ hours' cooking. Stew them gently in the melted butter. Dissolve the tomato purée in a glass of hot stock, and pour over the vegetables. Add the veal slices and more hot stock to cover. Cover and allow this sauce to reduce at moderate heat until it has become concentrated and thick and has mostly been absorbed by the meat. During this process it is advisable to check every fifteen minutes whether enough liquid remains, and to add more hot stock if necessary. When the meat falls away from the bone, after about 2½ hours, it is done. If the sauce is too thin, allow it to reduce a little more, uncovered. Like risotto, this is a

28

dish which calls for patient and attentive cooking if it is to succeed. You have to take the time to chop the vegetables finely, and stay in the kitchen and keep checking how much the sauce has reduced.

I know a publisher in Milan who thinks there is nothing to beat a risotto with delicate pigs' tails; he fondly remembers the risotto of his childhood, which was served with fried larks. The fashionable risotto creations of many Milan restaurants irritate him, and he says Champagne or strawberry risotto are snobbish masquerades. He gave me the recipe for frogs' leg risotto, which Eugenio Montale praised in a poem as a "triumph of Milanese cuisine". To understand the traditional place of frogs and rice in the country cooking of Lombardy and Piedmont, you only have to have seen the rice fields of the Po valley, where as far as the eye can see there is nothing but rice, the odd row of trees, and innumerable water channels, small and large, in which the frogs croak, the flies breed and fishermen with long rods hunt for frogs.

Risotto con le rane
Risotto with frogs' legs

500 g frogs, gutted and skinned
350 g rice
1 onion
1 bunch of parsley
1 clove of garlic
dry white wine
a little stock
salt and pepper

Remove the thighs, separating the meat from the tiny bones.
Cook the remaining parts of the frogs in a litre of salted water
until the liquid has reduced by a third; sieve and keep the
liquid warm. Then melt half the butter in a pan and gently fry
the thighs and the garlic, taking this out as soon as it begins to
turn brown. Sprinkle the meat with the finely-chopped parsley,
add a little meat stock and season with salt and pepper. In the
rest of the butter, gently fry the finely-chopped onion, add the
rice, maintaining the heat, add white wine, and cook the risotto
with the frog stock, adding this in small quantities while
stirring constantly. Once the risotto is al dente, *serve, adding a*
spoonful of the frog meat to each plate.

This risotto also tastes very good if the frogs' legs are just fried
with butter, parsley and garlic, without adding any meat stock,
and mixed in with the rice during the final minutes of cooking.

Butter, rather than olive oil, is used for cooking in Milan, as these recipes show. This is because of the Lombard milk industry, which produces almost a third of the milk in Italy. In addition, each year 24 hectolitres of milk are made into cheese: Grana, Parmesan, Gorgonzola, Robiola and Taleggio. This also includes the mild, white mascarpone, described by Alberto Savinio as a "compromise between butter and cream" and as the "capon among cheeses: a fat eunuch who renounces pleasure for pleasure's sake".

In Milan, mascarpone is made into a dessert that has become almost as well known to the north of the Alps under the name *tiramisù* (pick me up) as pizza is. But the best *crema di mascarpone* I have ever eaten was not in Milan, but with Yvonne in Zurich; she had the recipe from her English ex-husband, who runs a small hotel in Tuscany.

Crema di mascarpone (tiramisù)
Mascarpone cream

200 g langues de chat *(freshly baked if possible)*
200 g mascarpone
100 g sugar
3 eggs
2 tablespoons Marsala
2 tablespoons whisky
100–200 ml heavily sweetened coffee
plain chocolate, grated, or chocolate powder

Lay the biscuits out over a shallow dish and drizzle them with the chilled coffee. Beat the egg yolks and the sugar till fluffy, add the mascarpone, mix together well, and stir in the Marsala and the whisky. Then carefully fold in the whites, beaten till stiff, and pour the mixture over the biscuits, which should be completely covered. Finally, sprinkle with the powder or grated chocolate. (Brandy or rum may be used instead of whisky and Marsala).

There are so many good restaurants in Milan that everyone who knows the city well has his own favourites. One place that should not be missed is "Ciovassino", Via Ciovassino 5, not far from La Scala on the edge of the Brera. The ambience is just as pleasant and appealing as the little cobble-stone street that leads from the Via dell'Orso to the restaurant. Regular customers are clearly in the majority, and you can quickly see why, because if there is a table available, the service is so polite and good that you will decide to come back the next time you are in Milan. Here, just reading the menu is a pleasure, because there is such a rich variety of imaginative and surprising dishes. The starters, for instance, include long white little beans, called *cannellini*, that are served with scampi, or an incredible cep soup that develops its rich aroma under a crusty pastry lid. I also remember having roast pork with slices of quince, and a dessert consisting of fresh ricotta seasoned with the famous bitter honey from Sardinia.

Lunching at Ciovassino does not leave you sleepy or sluggish, but in just the right mood for a stroll to the Brera Museum, and you won't even mind if the galleries containing the great Italian masters of the past are closed on account of some new regulations or because there are not enough attendants. If you have less time, go back to the Via Manzoni and have a quick look at the Museo Poldi Pezzoli at number 12. The unique quality of this museum is that it is not a museum at all, but the home of the collector Gian Giacomo Poldi Pezzoli, which was bequeathed to the city of Milan in 1871. Everything has the charm of the personal touch; you see a French armchair and discover above it a Botticelli Madonna, and the heart beats faster as you go round this quiet palazzo where very little has changed for more than a hundred years.

Trieste,
or the inheritance of Maria Theresa

No guidebook will tell you that Trieste is a beautiful town. On the other hand, the poet Umberto Saba wrote in a famous verse of the "brittle grace" of his hometown. "Grazia scontrosa" – that is indeed an apposite characterisation of this port, which is today largely disused. There are not that many sights, few churches or treasures, scarcely a single museum worth visiting. Trieste is a relatively young town. Apart from the small mediaeval quarter, where a labyrinth of dark alleys lies beneath the cathedral of San Giusto, it was built as an Austrian free port between 1750 and 1850; during this period the population increased from five thousand to a hundred and twenty thousand. The generous harbour facilities, the spacious piazzas and the broad residential streets meeting at right angles mostly date form the reign of Maria Theresa, when Trieste developed into a cosmopolitan trading centre, attracting as immigrants Greeks, Armenians, Turks, Jews and Slovenes.

The severe and proud classicist architecture is an expression of the self-confidence of the merchants of Trieste. The old Exchange is a mighty palace with the façade of a Doric temple, a stone's throw away from the splendid main square, the Piazza Unità dell'Italia. Genuine locals still refer to this as the "Piazza Grande", with its expansive view of the sea; on many days throughout the year it is suffused with wind and a harsh light. This is also where the famous "Caffè degli specchi" is to be found, the early evening rendezvous of the elegant youth of Trieste, while during the day professors and pensioners read their paper amidst the middle-European nostalgia of its décor. The first time Lorenzo and I arrived in Trieste we found a fine old hotel not far from the railway station with a view of the harbour. It was only the next morning when bricks and mortar crashed down on to the floor in a corner of our room that we realized it was being rebuilt; they came from a hole in the roof through which, as we later found out, new pipes and cables were being fitted. But we didn't let this mishap put us off; we liked this dreamy, sleepy town with its unusual surprises.

It also helped that on our very first evening we had discovered a place to return to regularly, where good wine was served at long, clean wooden tables and you could strike up a conversation with the other customers. It was called "Al Re di Coppe", in the Via Geppa, near the station. At first we thought it was a Spanish bar, because sherry and port were served in wine glasses, and the *prosciutto crudo* was sliced fairly thickly with a knife, in the Spanish manner. But when our neighbours ordered tripe and goulash at about eleven o'clock, we realised that this was a place in the true local style. No other town in Italy has so many pubs and so-called "buffets" where sauerkraut, sausages and boiled meat are sold; every menu includes goulash and tripe, and apple strudel, damson dumplings, *Guglhupf* and *Sachertorte* are among the most popular desserts.

The landlord of the "Re di Coppe" was not from Spain or from Trieste; he was called Marioq Vellic and came from Istria. His sister Carmela was responsible for the kitchen, and at first she was reluctant to tell me the secret of her delicate, light and tasty tripe, because she thought it was far too simple, not really a recipe at all, but just boiled tripe. But I managed to talk her round, and tripe *alla triestina* has been one of my favourite recipes ever since.

Busecca alla triestina
Tripe alla triestina

Ingredients for six:
1 kg tripe
2 tablespoons olive oil
40 g white bacon fat
40 g bacon, diced
2–3 medium onions
3–5 cloves of garlic
salt and pepper

Put the olive oil and the bacon and fat in a frying pan and warm them through. Then gently fry the finely-chopped onions golden yellow, add the garlic and the tripe; fry until they have released all their liquid and are beginning to take on colour. This will take a good ten minutes, and is essential if the dish is to be successful. Then add hot water to cover the tripe, put the lid on, and leave to boil 1½–2 hours at low heat. They taste excellent warmed up too.

Another aspect of Trieste's subtle charm is the close symbiosis between town and country. Whether you arrive by train or by car, you always find you reach the centre surprisingly fast, because unlike towns of a similar size – its population today is 240,000 – Trieste is not surrounded by an anonymous and ugly industrial zone. Reaching the high plains of the town's Slovenian hinterland, a range of *karst* hills, is just as quick: it is a desolate landscape with low-lying but vigorous vegetation, a rich alpine flora and little farming villages where you can drink the dark, flavoursome vino terrano with prosciutto crudo in inns with no sign to proclaim their trade. We also visited one of the many limestone grottos, where you clamber in small groups on steep iron ladders and along narrow paths between fairytale pink and emerald stalagmites and stalactites.

On our way back we stopped at a little garden restaurant above the town where we sat on a gravelled terrace beneath plane trees and admired the view of the Gulf of Trieste. Along with the white wine and mineral water we had ordered, a young girl brought us a plateful of pieces of flat omelette filled with aromatic herbs and vegetables. To be precise, it was a *frittata* rather than an omelette, the Italian name for this simple variant of the French version: it is just made from beaten eggs, with no milk or flour, combined with cooked vegetables, pasta, fish or meat and fried like a pancake. It was in Trieste that I discovered that a vegetable omelette almost tastes better cold, and since then, instead of salted almonds and olives with the aperitif, I have occasionally served a *fertae cu lis ierbuzzis*, as the dish is called in the dialect of Trieste.

Frittata alle erbe
Herb omelette

Ingredients for four (as a starter):
a handful of spinach or Swiss chard
1 leek
2 medium onions
freshly picked basil and sage
2 tablespoons chopped parsley
8 tablespoons olive oil
8 eggs
salt and pepper

Slice the leek and onion and boil for a few minutes in a little salted water; leave to drain in a sieve. Heat 4 tablespoons of olive oil in a pan, add the boiled vegetables, the spinach, sliced into strips, and the herbs and leave to stew on low heat for ten minutes. Whisk the eggs, season, and combine with the herbs and vegetables. Heat the remaining 4 tablespoons olive oil in the pan, add the egg and vegetable mixture and fry till golden yellow, shaking the pan continually. Slide the frittata on to a pan lid or a flat plate and turn it over so it can be fried on the other side, on low heat. The egg should be completely set.

Frittata may been eaten warm or cold; to serve cold as a starter, cut into eight pieces like a cake. Peas, carrots, cauliflower, green beans, courgettes etc. may be used instead of the vegetables in the recipe. Fresh mint also goes well with this dish.

Unfortunately, the good quality of life in Trieste is due to the fact that it is a dying town; unification with Italy led to economic ruin. The population of Trieste is constantly falling. The young move away, and more than half of the inhabitants are retired. Daniele del Giudice's novel about Bobi Balzen, a figure from Trieste's literary scene – published in German as "The land as seen from the sea" – is a subtle and merciless portrayal of the well-preserved and ageing town with its Hapsburg nostalgia. He sits with old men in literary cafés and gets women who once inspired poems by Eugenio Montale to show him their photo albums; he observes the streets, where there are a remarkable number of old-fashioned cars, and the harbour: "I walk along the immaculate quays, totally shipshape, and you are not allowed to park anywhere. You can see they remove the seaweed every so often, with acid. The fact that there is not a single ship makes this level of upkeep all the more impressive. Nothing is decaying, not even the sleepers or the arms of the cranes, bent over like birds' wings. It looks as though the maritime world had suddenly been amputated from the town, with only the neat surgically finished stump to show it had ever been there."

Late one afternoon I visited the second hand bookshop at 30 Via San

Nicolò, owned until 1957 by Umberto Saba. I entered a low-ceilinged room leading on to several other small rooms, all of them stuffed with old books, music and engravings. In a corner there was a gigantic photo of Saba in old age, slender and dressed entirely in black. Somewhere a typewriter clattered. I followed the sound and found a pale old man who I thought was just like Saba. But he quickly explained to me that he had nothing to do with the Saba family; he just bought the bookshop from them. To change the subject I asked whether there were any books on the cuisine of Trieste. Then he relaxed and said that was a large topic; he told me he had been writing a cookbook for years. He began singing the praises of the local cuisine, which – so he claimed – organically adapts recipes of Venetian, Austrian, Hungarian, Greek, Jewish and Slavic origin to the elegant style of Trieste. Almost every dish contains paprika or pepper, he continued, marjoram and cumin are extensively used, smoked bacon is used in preference to unsmoked, and the nutritious foundation of every menu is not pasta, rice or polenta, but hearty soups that combine starchy ingredients like beans, lentils, dried peas, rice, corn, barley, potatoes and pasta with bacon, sausages or spare ribs to make a meal in themselves. These minestrones, he went on, could contain vegetables like carrots, celeriac, leeks, or spinach, and in the winter cabbage, sauerkraut or pickled beets, marinated in marc for thirty days. I listened so attentively that he fetched one of his favourite recipes from the box where he kept them and let me copy it down.

Minestra di fagioli
Trieste bean soup
200 g dried white or speckled beans
30 g smoked bacon
celery leaves

1 large potato
1 carrot
1 large onion
1–2 cloves of garlic
2 sage leaves
1 bunch of parsley
1 bay leaf
salt and pepper

Soak the beans for at least 24 hours in cold water, drain and heat up with a little water. As soon as the water comes to the boil, pour it off. Now place the beans with 1¾ litres hot water in a saucepan with the celery, carrot, potato and the bay leaf; simmer on low heat until the beans are soft. Remove the potato and the carrot, mash them up with a fork and put them back in. Remove the bay leaf and season. Gently fry the finely-chopped bacon, parsley, onion, garlic and sage in a pan till thoroughly cooked; add to the soup at the end of cooking, stir well and simmer for another few minutes.

This is one of the tastiest bean soups I know. The mashed potato makes it so thick that there is no need to add any pasta, as is done in other parts of Italy. No bread is usually eaten with this soup either.

I last visited Trieste a few years ago with a friend from the Ticino radio station, who had arranged an interview with Fulvio Tomizza. We visited the writer in his Istrian village, forty kilometres to the south of Trieste, where he lives in a simple stone house with no telephone. Behind olive trees and green willows, the sea was visible in the distance. We sat in the shade of young chestnut and lime trees planted by Tomizza himself and drank the cool aromatic white wine of the previous year. Although the great round stone on which the glasses stood came from an old oil press, the atmosphere was not idyllic; the beautiful landscape was just the backdrop to a conversation dealing with concrete ways of improving for the present and the future the dialogue between Slovenes, Croats and Italians that has been taking place in this border territory for centuries.

On the way back we stopped in a fish restaurant in Muggia where we ordered crispy fried scampi, a dish which splendidly applies the Austrian tradition of frying in breadcrumbs to natural Mediterranean ingredients. Fried chicken, Wiener schnitzel, and breaded cauliflower or breaded courgettes are a popular feature of Trieste cuisine.

Scampi dorati
Fried scampi

700 g scampi tails (fresh or frozen)
a little flour
2 eggs
breadcrumbs
olive oil, salt
1 lemon

Dry the scampi carefully, dredge them in the flour and then in the beaten and salted eggs, and finally in the breadcrumbs. Fry in plenty of olive oil. Drain briefly on kitchen paper and serve as hot as possible, garnished with lemon slices.

Rather than salad, the scampi were served with a dark green, pungent vegetable with crispy diced bacon. We were surprised when the owner told us this was *radicchio* or *cicorino verde*, the pale green and slightly bitter salad enjoyed throughout northern Italy, normally cut into very thin strips. For those who are not fond of bitter flavours, this cooked salad dish can also be made with prickly lettuce.

Cicoria con pancetta affiumicata
Cooked salad with smoked bacon

1 kg prickly lettuce or radicchio
olive oil
salt and pepper
50 g diced bacon

*Fry the bacon in hot olive oil till translucent, add the washed
vegetable, season, turn the heat down very low, cover the pan
and steam gently for ten to fifteen minutes till done.*

The affinity of fried bacon with firm, somewhat bitter salads is also shown
by the usual way of serving dandelion leaves in France; in the spring they
are dressed with diced bacon, a little vinegar and salt. The same accompaniment also goes with green or red radicchio salad.

Venetian sardines

It was the end of May in Pavia, where I was visiting Felix, who taught there. Both of us had the time and inclination to see a bit more of Italy, and Felix suggested Venice as our destination. I did not know Venice then and didn't really have any desire to. In my view, I had already seen so many pictures of the great museum that was Venice that there was no need for me to actually go there, especially as I had no interest in museum-piece towns. But I was ready to have a brief look at the place, and as soon as, from the bridge just past Mestre, we caught sight of the luminous grey silhouette of the city rising out of the sea with its churches and palaces, I began to suspect that my theory about Venice was wrong. By the time I was gazing out of our hotel room window at the quiet canal and the crumbling façades of the old houses, and could hear the hubbub of the voices of passers by with no traffic noise to drown them out, I was already enchanted by Venice. It's not the churches, the palaces and the works of art that make this city so incomparable, but the absence of modern technology; it shows how beautiful a town built for people can be – pedestrians ambling and strolling, or stopping to chat, because the streets belong to them and are their own space. Then there is the attraction of the water, the silent gliding of boats on the canals, the gentle lapping of waves on old walls and the delicate, bright light that descends on the city from the sea.

That first evening we ate at the "Pergola", a small trattoria near the La Fenice theatre. We were amazed at the many different kinds of risotto listed on the menu. There was risotto with shrimps, scampi, mussels, fish,

43

chicken livers, chicken, quail, mushrooms, fennel, peas, courgettes, artichokes and asparagus. It was as if there were no delicacies on sea or on land that could not be turned into a risotto. This liking for rice has its roots in the history of the maritime republic of Venice; through its trade with the orient it had adopted rice from the Arabs as early as the high middle ages, long before it was introduced to Lombardy by the Spaniards in the sixteenth century. It is in Venice that the multiplicity of Italian rice dishes was developed. Felix ordered the famous rice dish called *risi e bisi* – *bisi* from *piselli*, peas – which is a creamy risotto with a light green colour that comes from fresh young peas. I decided to have the *risotto con zucchine*, still one of my favourite dishes, not least because it delights the eye as much as the palate; instead of disintegrating as you might expect, the green slices of courgette, cooked with the rice from the start, keep their elegant shape and remain *al dente*, as it were, like the rice.

Risotto con zucchine
Risotto with courgettes

500 g young small courgettes
50 g diced bacon
1 clove of garlic
1 small onion
2 tablespoons butter
salt and pepper
400 g rice
1¼ litres meat stock
50 g grated Parmesan
1 tablespoon chopped parsley

Slice the washed courgettes and finely chop the onion and garlic.

44

*Then heat one tablespoon of butter to fry the bacon till
translucent; add the garlic and onion and stew till pale yellow.
Add the sliced courgettes and fry them until they are golden
yellow, stirring frequently. Add the rice, fry well and gradually
add the boiling stock so that the rice remains at a constant simmer.
After approximately twenty minutes, once the rice is al dente, mix
it with the rest of the butter, the Parmesan and the parsley.*

Many years later, I was on the island of San Giorgio one December for a congress of the Fondazione Cini. The island has a panoramic view of Venice. Our lunch in the former Benedictine monastery began with a *risotto al radicchio rosso* that was so delectably tasty that I asked the maître d'hôtel for the recipe. I ended up having a talk with the cook, who not only gave me his recipe but also explained the difference between the round red *radicchio di Chioggia*, used in salads, and the *radicchio di Treviso*, whose long leaves are mainly cooked as a vegetable because of their more intense flavour.

Risotto al radicchio rosso
Risotto with radicchio

1 small onion
300 g red radicchio
2 tablespoons olive oil
1 tablespoon butter
400 g rice
150 ml milk
meat stock
100 ml cream
5–6 tablespoons grated Parmesan

Heat the butter and oil in a saucepan, cook the chopped onion till yellow and add the radicchio, *cut into fine strips. Gently fry them till they lose their red colour, add the rice and fry, stirring vigorously. Add the milk, which tempers the strong flavour of the* radicchio. *Now gradually add the hot stock, stirring constantly and always waiting till the liquid has been fully absorbed. Add the cream and the Parmesan after approximately twenty minutes, once the rice is* al dente. *Leave the rice to stand, covered, for 2–3 minutes before serving, to allow all the ingredients to blend thoroughly together.*

My tired, aching feet told me on the very first evening that Venice is a city for pedestrians. The next morning, I bought a pair of flat espadrilles in a little shop next to the hotel; after that, I had no more problems. Felix and I walked for hours in the narrow streets, called *calli*, through *campi* and *campielli*, the little squares punctuating the main routes through the city like pauses for breath, and over many of the four hundred bridges that link together the islands on which Venice is built. On these trips we soon discovered that the stream of tourists is concentrated in the streets and alleys around the Piazza San Marco, and the other areas of the city belong almost exclusively to the inhabitants. Seeing the garbage collection boat making its way slowly along a minor canal with a little vessel heavily laden with green watermelons coming the other way, you suddenly understand why it is that there are innumerable canals in Venice without a particular name, whereas not a single street corner is anonymous; every courtyard or passageway, every cul-de-sac and the merest hint of a square all have a precise appellation. Whatever is differentiated from the unifying surrounding element, water, has its own unique identity, is called Calle, Salizzada, Lista, Ramo, Corte, Sottoportego, Riva, Fondamenta, Campo or Campiello. The incomparable wealth of Venetian street names draws with proud assurance on dialect: it is "Sottoportego", not "Sottoportico"; "San Zulian", not "San Giuliano". Venetian has been spoken for a thousand years, after all, but the standard language of Italy is six hundred years old at most.

It is probably because Venice is a city of pedestrians that there are so many places to rest and rally your strength. If you have lost your way amid the labyrinth of alleys, or if you are simply tired from walking in the fresh sea air, you will soon find a little bar or café where the *Tocai di Lison*, Venice's light, well-balanced white wine, is waiting for the customers behind the counter in great wicker-bound bottles. There is also usually a *soppressa*, a delicate, tasty salami, waiting on a wooden board. You can sit with your wine and sausage at a large wooden table; there will be less to pay for this convivial snack than for one of the hotdogs sold to tourists with a sprig of rosemary at the stalls near the Piazza San Marco.

The true meaning of Venetian cuisine is something you only come to recognize gradually. To enjoy its simple riches fully, those who do not live on the coast must understand that in a city built on thousands of stilts in the sea, fish and seafood are bound to be the principal foodstuff, which have been the foundation of the Venetian diet for 1,500 years; to this day the fish consumption of Venice remains the highest of any Italian city. If you go to Venice, you need to forget about chops and steaks, roasts and cutlets, beef, pork and lamb, and set your sights on eating healthy fish from the sea. Only by resolving to endure the monotony of a cuisine based entirely on fish can you discover the fabulous wealth of Venetian food, which depends entirely on the high quality of fresh natural ingredients. The wide range of fish, molluscs and crustaceans in the Adriatic can be admired every morning at the fish market by the Rialto bridge. Stylish blue-black sea salmon lie next to cases of shining silver sardines and mountains of round, oval, heart-shaped mussels, both smooth and rough, and the long-armed white octopuses and the bizarre toad crabs are a fascinating sight.

Not far from the Rialto bridge is one of the best fish restaurants in Venice, the "Trattoria alla Madonna". It is a large, bright place, decorated in typical Italian plain style, with adroit and friendly waiters who know how to give undecided customers intelligent and competent advice. This is the most direct introduction to Italian fish cookery. It is more or less obligatory to have an *antipasto di mare* as the first course, a delicious collection of crustaceans and mussels served with just a few slices of lemon and a pepper mill filled with white peppercorns. Or if you prefer, there is the *risotto di pesce*, a risotto mixed with delicate nuggets of fish. Naturally, the main course will be based on fish too, the best and freshest fish, brushed with olive oil and grilled on a charcoal stove. There would be no point at all in asking for it to be cooked any other way. Fish sauces are as foreign to Venetian cookery as boiled fish. A good fish should be grilled, *e basta*. Smaller, cheaper varieties of fish such as sardines or anchovies may be fried, or else braised with wine and herbs.

The most famous Venetian recipe for sardines is for *sarde in soar*, or sardines marinated with lots of chopped onions, which are served as a starter or snack. Any other fried fish or fish leftovers may be pickled in vinegar according to the same recipe; in this way they will keep for several days.

Sarde in soar
Venetian marinated sardines

600 g fresh sardines
600 g onions
flour
olive oil
white wine vinegar

Gut the sardines and cut off their heads, then wash and dry well. Turn them in the flour, fry in the hot oil till crispy, drain on kitchen paper and sprinkle with salt. Pour away the frying oil, wipe the pan out with kitchen paper and heat half a glass of olive oil in it. Add the chopped onions, frying, covered, very gently till golden yellow. Now add two glasses of vinegar and simmer for a few minutes. Fill a ceramic pot with sardines in layers, covering each layer with onions and the hot broth. The

marinade must eventually completely cover the fish. Cover with
a lid or with foil and keep in a cool place – cellar or fridge – for
at least a day. The marinated sardines may then be served as a
starter or main course. They can be kept for two weeks as they
are.

Note: In old Venetian recipes, the marinade also includes
pine kernels and raisins, pre-soaked in warm water.

This combination of fish and onions, which seems rather odd to us, is very common in Venetian cooking. This may have something to do with the medicinal properties of onions in combating infection, especially important in a port where sickness and plague were frequently introduced. For this reason, "*alla veneziana*" simply means "cooked with onions"; this also applies to the famous *fegato alla veneziana*, or Venetian calves' liver. The only Venetian thing about it is the onion, whereas in fish-rich Venice, calves' liver is an import, and does not even appear on the menu of simple establishments. That does not stop the Americans who feast on soft buttery liver *alla veneziana* in "Harry's Bar", served with onions stewed in half oil, half butter; this is entirely in keeping with the international tradition of a city which was happy, as Marco Polo said, to try out everything which came from the Greeks, the Saracens and the Chinese, and keep the best.

The best place to find good cheap local food is in the workers' and fishermen's bars on the island of Giudecca; to get there, take vaporetto number 5 from Riva degli Schiavoni. One family business, for example, is the trattoria "L'Altanella" near the Sant'Eufemia stop. It is in a street that is so narrow that you can touch the walls of the houses on both sides if you stretch your arms out. Signora Paola's *fritto misto* is unsurpassed, and her secret is that she does not coat the little fish, scampi and calamari in flour, because she firmly believes that flour hampers the formation by the fish and oil of a crispy surface. Another speciality of the house is the *spaghetti alle acciughe*, served with a tasty sauce made of salted anchovies and lots of onions.

Finally, I once ate another sardine dish here, which derives from the haute cuisine of the maritime republic of Venice. It consists of fresh sardines braised with orange juice, olives and pine kernels.

Sarde all'arancia
Sardines with orange juice

1 kg fresh sardines
salt
olive oil
3 juicy oranges
100 g green olives
30 g pine kernels
1 glass of white wine
pepper
40 g breadcrumbs

Wash the sardines, remove the heads, and gut them, also carefully removing the backbones. Then cut their tails off, dry them thoroughly and salt them. Pour two tablespoons of olive oil into an ovenproof dish and cover with a layer of sardines. Peel the oranges and slice them thinly. Stone the olives and cut in strips. Then cover the sardines with a layer of orange slices and olive strips, sprinkling a few pine kernels in the gaps. Pour olive oil and wine over them and add freshly milled pepper. Continue adding layers of sardines covered with orange slices, olives and pine kernels until all the ingredients have been used up. Finally, sprinkle the breadcrumbs over the sardines, pour plenty of olive oil on top and put the dish in a preheated oven; bake the sardines for thirty minutes on medium heat until golden brown.

The vegetable and herb cookery
of Liguria

What I think is the most beautiful train journey in Italy runs from Genoa to La Spezia, where I have often gone on holiday. There is little risk in giving away La Spezia's secret as a summer holiday destination – the charm of this little port is so discreet that there is no fear of an invasion of tourists, as in the neighbouring Cinque Terre, where almost as much German as Italian can be heard in the spring and summer. But in La Spezia there are hardly any tourists even in July and August, just hotels with vacancies, peaceful streets and trattorias with friendly waiters and careful cooks. Besides the many little steamers that can take you to the beautiful beaches of Lerici, Fiascherino, Porto Venere and Palmaria, there is the train to the Cinque Terre, where the cliffs descend so steeply to the sea that for almost the entire trip you are going through tunnels, and the sea can only be glimpsed from the stations. It is the alternation between the darkness of the tunnels and the clear light of the coast that gives the line all the way to Genoa its particular attraction. This railway was built along the coast a century ago, with more than a hundred tunnels, and it is very popular with children and trainspotters. In the Cinque Terre the railway provides the only link between the five villages, and even on the hottest of summer days a refreshing breeze blows out of the old fashioned tunnel entrances over the little railway stations.

Just how much of a short-cut these tunnels are becomes apparent on the path from one village to the next, which leads uphill and down through vineyards, sunlit woods, deep ravines and valleys. Many years ago Felix and I walked from Manarola to Vernazza via Corniglia; we arrived at around noon, hungry and thirsty. We found a trattoria in a shady side street, and we sat at one of the three tables next to the door, where a pleasant current of air allowed us to forget the midday heat. The waiter – in fact, it was the owner – suggested the *sardine alla casalinga*, home-made sardines, which his wife had just cooked. That was what we ordered, and we did not regret it. It was a gratin with potatoes, courgettes and lots of garlic, a dish that could only be invented by people for whom fish is a daily staple to be turned with imagination and love into a filling meal.

Sardine alla casalinga
Home-made sardines

500 g potatoes, boiled in their skins
250 g courgettes
250 g tomatoes
3–4 cloves of garlic
500 g fresh sardines
1 tablespoon breadcrumbs
olive oil
salt and pepper

Peel the boiled potatoes, which should not be too well done, and slice them; with the slices cover the base of a well-oiled ovenproof dish. Sprinkle them with salt and pepper and the chopped garlic. Next comes a layer of thinly sliced courgette and tomatoes, skinned and quartered. Season again before adding the final layer of the gratin, the sardines. Head and gut them, drizzle with lemon juice, season inside and out and place on top

of the bed of potatoes and vegetables. Sprinkle them with
breadcrumbs, pour plenty of olive oil on top and bake in a
medium oven for a good half hour.

We washed down the sardine gratin in Vernazza with the white wine that ripens in the Cinque Terre vineyards hanging above the sea. We drank this dry, flavoursome and rather full-bodied wine with the meat and cheese as well as with the fish; its effects can be felt for the rest of the day, and all of the different kinds, their flavours subtly reflecting their particular origin, are truly good wines, and don't give you a headache. What's more, it costs almost nothing. In those days you could drink four small glasses of it in the cellar bar "Zio Bramante" in Manarola for a hundred lire. The wine stood on each table in wicker bottles, and it was the customers who kept count of how many glasses they had had. When I gave Felix a rather surprised look as he poured himself yet another glass, he explained that there was no way he could give the landlord less than a hundred lire.

We struck up a conversation with this landlord, an athletic man with a grey beard who looked like a retired pirate. He told us about the isolated villages on the wooded slopes of the Apennines that hardly a single tourist ever reached, let alone a group of walkers. We followed his advice to turn our backs on the sea for once, and in the midst of the empty forest scented with pine resin we discovered the trattoria "Davidin" – which means "little David" – where you could sit on a terrace in the evening breeze and enjoy local dishes at a reasonable price. My favourite was the Ligurian rabbit, which derives its special flavour from olives, rosemary and the chopped liver of the animal. I later got the recipe from Dina, who grew up in Chiavari.

Coniglio alla ligure
Ligurian rabbit

1 young rabbit
1 glass of olive oil
2 cloves of garlic
1 sprig of rosemary
2 glasses of red wine
1 ripe tomato
50–100 g stoned olives

Have the rabbit cut into pieces of a size suitable for stewing; fry gently in a pan for five minutes until they have released all their liquid. Then heat up the oil in a saucepan, fry the rabbit pieces, and add the rosemary leaves and garlic after chopping them finely together, as well as the diced rabbit liver, followed by the red wine. Then season, cover and allow the rabbit to simmer for about an hour and a half until done. Should the liquid threaten to boil dry altogether, moisten with a little stock. After 45 minutes, add the chopped and skinned tomato and the olives. The sauce should eventually be quite thick and rich, with very little liquid remaining.

It was also at the "Davidin" that we first ate the Ligurian *castagnaccio*, a crusty pancake made from chestnut flour and sprinkled with rosemary needles and pine kernels. Just as in Ticino, Friuli and the Veneto, in the Ligurian mountains chestnuts were once one of the greatest assets of the peasants. Apart from wood for heating and building, they provided flour for day-to-day eating. Chestnut cakes are an example of simple country baking which does not need to rise and so requires neither yeast nor baking powder. They are not really sweet, so they go just as well with a glass of wine or an espresso. They are easy and quick to make.

Castagnaccio
Chestnut cake

500 g chestnut flour (from health food shops or Italian grocers)
3 tablespoons sugar
olive oil
milk
2 tablespoons pine kernels
2 tablespoons sultanas (soaked in tepid water)
fennel seeds
salt

Sieve the chestnut flour into a basin so that there will be no lumps later on, add a pinch of salt together with the sugar and mix in enough olive oil to make a smooth, firm dough, stirring vigorously; then dilute this by gradually adding milk and combine with the pine kernels and sultanas. Brush a baking dish well with olive oil and fill with the mixture; sprinkle with fennel seeds and drizzle a few tablespoons of olive oil over it. Bake in a medium oven for about 45 minutes.

No discussion of Ligurian cooking would be complete without singing the praises of *pesto alla genovese*, which represents a kind of quintessence of the simple yet sophisticated cuisine of this coastal province. *Pesto* – the word is derived from *pestare*, to crush – is a sauce made of basil, garlic, pine kernels and cheese ground up in a mortar and combined with olive oil. It has an incredibly intense flavour and a beautiful dark green colour.

It is mixed with boiling hot al dente spaghetti or *trenette*, the name of the pasta used for this dish in Genoa. Here is the original Genoese recipe:

Pesto alla genovese
Basil and garlic sauce

1–2 bunches of fresh basil
5 cloves of garlic
1 handful of pine kernels
½ teaspoon salt
1 tablespoon grated Pecorino sardo (strongly flavoured Sardinian sheep's milk cheese)
1 tablespoon grated Parmesan
8 tablespoons high quality olive oil

Roughly chop the pine kernels with the garlic and crush them in a marble or earthenware mortar. Chop up the basil leaves and crush them with the salt (so that they retain their colour), also in the mortar. Finally, add the grated cheese and gradually stir in the oil to make a creamy sauce. Before the pesto is mixed with the drained spaghetti, it should be made somewhat smoother and runnier by adding 2–3 tablespoons of the cooking water. To round off the balance of flavours, some housewives add a piece of fresh butter to the warmed dish.

According to Ligurian tradition, pesto should be crushed in a mortar. This is certainly the best method, but I know from experience that pesto can also be made successfully in a blender if the chopped ingredients are processed with the oil on the slowest setting. There are also variations in the possible ingredients; depending on whether a mild or strong flavour is preferred, just Parmesan may be used or just pecorino, or a less strongly flavoured sheep cheese from the same area. The pine kernels may be replaced by walnuts, blanched in water and then skinned. Pesto also tastes delicious without any nuts at all. The most important thing is the quality of the basil, so there is no point making pesto in the winter with flavourless imported greenhouse basil. Pesto sold in jars is not much good either. As long you are careful to ensure that it is always covered by a layer of olive oil, home-made pesto will keep in the fridge for no more than 3–4 days.

Few tourists have any idea how real spaghetti, or *trenette al pesto*, are prepared in the Genoese family kitchen, because they are now only found on the menu in a few tradition-conscious restaurants. It was many years ago with a Swiss family in Genoa that I ate them for the first time, and to this day they have remained a kind of talisman for the healthy and simple yet at the same time sophisticated qualities of Italian cuisine.

Spaghetti col pesto alla genovese
Genoese pesto with spaghetti

400 g spaghetti
100 g tender green beans
2 medium potatoes
pesto (see preceding recipe)
grated pecorino

Cut the peeled potatoes into small cubes and boil for five minutes in salted water. Then add the spaghetti and the beans, finely chopped; boil together till the pasta is al dente. *Drain*

*and mix the pasta with the pesto in a warmed bowl so that the
cheese melts and the pesto communicates its flavour to the
spaghetti, the potatoes and the beans. Serve with grated
pecorino. Several alterations can be made to this dish: for
example, the potatoes may be omitted, or small courgettes may
be cooked together with the beans.*

There is a second excellent pasta sauce in Liguria, made like pesto with a pestle and mortar, namely *salsa di noci*, walnut sauce; it is light and creamy with a delicate, slightly bitter nutty flavour. It is the classic accompaniment for *pansoti*, the three-cornered ravioli of the region, filled with herbs and ricotta. The reason it has not become as well-known as pesto may well be that it is time-consuming to make, because not only must the walnuts be cracked, but the brown skins must be removed from the nuts by blanching them. Such painstaking treatment of natural produce is one of the key qualities of Italian country cooking. (My friend from Chiavari also taught me that minestrone has a better flavour if, in the summer, the fresh bean seeds are peeled before being added to the soup; this means laboriously pulling the skin of each individual bean by hand to make the minestrone tasty, nutritious and smooth.)

Salsa di noci
Walnut sauce

*500 g walnuts
1 clove of garlic
3 tablespoons of olive oil
two crustless rolls
200 ml milk
100 ml cream*

salt
pepper

Soak the rolls in the milk, squeeze them out and place in the mortar together with the shelled and peeled walnuts, the peeled garlic clove and a little salt. Crush everything together into a smooth paste, then mix with olive oil and cream to create a sauce of thick consistency; season with finely chopped fresh marjoram.

A conversation I had with a young cook from Moneglia revealed that even once sacrosanct culinary traditions are being questioned; he told me that he makes pesto for his customers without garlic, using just basil, pine kernels and pecorino. For him, the walnut sauce is quickly made by whizzing up unpeeled nuts in the blender with cream.

Why Parmesan goes with almost everything

I have always felt a particular affinity for the cuisine of Parma, with its emphasis on butter and cheese. As a student the only meal I knew how to cook was spaghetti, which I mixed with plenty of grated Parmesan and butter, and I remained faithful to this simple and effective combination later on, when I had learned how to cook. There is nothing I prefer to vegetables *alla parmigiana*; what could be better than broccoli, fennel, leek, cauliflower and asparagus boiled in salted water and served with grated Parmesan and melted butter? Yet it surprised me when Lorenzo reached for the cheese grater one evening when we were having dinner together and sprinkled Parmesan on the spinach. He explained to me that in northern Italy, Parmesan and spinach go together just as much as Parmesan and spaghetti, indeed it is used as a sort of universal condiment. He told me of a dream that was a more poetical illustration of the universal significance of Parmesan than any comparison: he had once dreamed that his watch was so utterly beyond repair that the watchmaker said there was nothing to be done. Then he opened the watch, sprinkled a pinch of Parmesan into it – and it began to tick once more.

It is only when it melts that grated Parmesan develops its full flavour, whether in hot broth, risotto just before it is served, or on top of butter with hot butter poured over it. This also happens when a dish is finished off under the grill, a method I specially like with spinach.

Spinaci alla parmigiana
Spinach topped with grilled Parmesan

1 kg spinach
50 g butter
salt and pepper
100 g grated Parmesan

Clean and wash the spinach and place in a pan on medium heat. Cook for one or two minutes till done. There will be enough water left on the leaves – boiling in salted water would make the spinach lose flavour and colour. Then rinse with cold water and press out thoroughly, preferably by hand. Chop on a wooden board. Season and heat through briefly with 20 g butter; leave to cool on a plate. Twenty minutes before eating, grease an ovenproof glass dish with butter and put the spinach in it, dotting it with little pieces of butter and adding plenty of grated Parmesan before placing in a medium oven. After a quarter of an hour, when the cheese forms a golden crust, the spinach will be hot and ready to serve.

Grilled meat may be eaten with this spinach; or I will have vegetables *alla parmigiana* with just bread and wine as a light supper.

What makes Parmesan different from other grating cheeses is that it melts without forming threads like Emmental or Gruyère. It simply dissolves in broth, minestrone or risotto and imparts a delicate, creamy consistency. But one of the basic rules of Italian cooking is that you should not buy grated Parmesan, but grate it yourself shortly before eating; when waiters in good restaurants grate Parmesan straight on to your risotto like truffle, they are not being pretentious, because this really does taste better than grated cheese that has been hanging around for hours or even days.

Parmesan is also an excellent dessert cheese; with the cheese knife you cut big flakes – in Italian they are called *scaglie* – from ripe straw-yellow Parmesan, and allow them to dissolve between tongue and palate, where they release their mild, aromatic flavour.

I first visited the town from which Parmesan gets its name on my way to Rome. I found a room in the Hotel Stendhal, opposite the imposing Palazzo della Pilotta, and phoned up Baldassare Molossi, a schoolfriend of Luigi Malerba, editor of the *Gazzetta di Parma* and the author of a book on Parma's cuisine. We arranged to meet in the "Aurora", a restaurant where I got to know the cooking of this town in theory and in practice, beginning with the starter, which simply consisted of the two finest local delicacies: the mild and flavourful Parma ham, served in the "Aurora' without the fat, and *culatello*, a speciality of the surrounding countryside. It is the best part of the ham, weighing only four or five kilos, salted in a string net and transported to the Po valley to mature, where there is fog all through the winter. It is this damp climate, which lends the *culatello* its exquisite aromatic delicacy; Molossi told me that Gabriele D'Annunzio was addicted to it. Anyone who visits Parma should definitely try this speciality or, better still, take one home with them. In Parma, as in the whole province of Emilia, Lambrusco is drunk with food, a sparkling dry red wine that is responsible for the hearty appetite of the local gourmets; it makes the richest foods light and digestible.

In Emilia, a first course of pasta is practically compulsory. No other province has a greater wealth of special varieties of pasta. This is evident even in the streets of the town during the day, where you continually come across shops with windows piled high with home-made lasagne, noodles and spaghetti, tortellini, anolini and ravioli, enticingly egg-yellow or spinach-green. My expert guide advised me to order a mixture of *tortelli di zucca* and *tortelli di erbette*, large paper-thin ravioli filled with a mixture of pumpkin and cheese and, in the second case, ricotta and finely chopped Swiss chard. They are served, of course, with grated Parmesan and melted butter. For the meat course I picked *involtini*, a sort of roulade made of thin pieces of veal sprinkled with grated Parmesan and covered with a slice of Parma ham before being rolled up and stewed in a rich vegetable sauce. Molossi gave me a rough idea of the recipe, and I fine-tuned it back at home.

Involtini all'emiliana
Roulades all'emiliana

400 g thin slices of loin of veal
80 g grated Parmesan
100 g Parma ham
for the sauce:
30 g butter
50 g bacon
1 carrot
a few celery leaves
1 bunch of parsley
1 onion
1 small tin peeled tomatoes
1 tablespoon of tomato purée
2–3 sage leaves
1 tablespoon cognac
1 glass red or white wine
100–200 ml meat stock

Sprinkle grated Parmesan over the veal slices, cover with Parma ham, roll and secure with a toothpick. For the sauce, chop the carrot, celery, onion and parsley. Then melt the butter in a cast-iron pan, add the diced bacon and fry till translucent. Now add the roulades, frying them slowly on each side until golden

brown. Remove them from the pan, warm the vegetables
through and return the roulades to the pan. Turn the heat up
slightly and add the cognac, followed gradually by the wine.
Wait until all the liquid has evaporated before adding the
tomatoes, sage leaves and the tomato purée, stirred with a little
hot stock; add a little more stock. Then cover the pan and leave
to simmer for an hour on very low heat.

In Parma we ate these roulades with spinach, but at home I
find fluffy mashed potato is the best accompaniment.

At the table next to us a whole group of elegantly dressed young people were having such a lively conversation that I couldn't help hearing that they were talking about Maria Freni's performance in the latest production of *Don Carlos* at La Scala. My host told me that in Parma, the two topics of conversation are food and music. The classical Teatro Regio is not just one of the prettiest theatres in northern Italy, it is also famous for the audience, which whistles in response to any note that is sung even slightly off key; here it is still possible for an opera to fold with a theatrical scandal, leading to despairing sopranos refusing to keep on singing their parts. It's probably no accident that Arturo Toscanini and Ildebrando Pizzetti come from Parma, nor that Giuseppe Verdi was born in the town and then lived nearby, nor that Niccolò Paganini's imposing sarcophagus is in Parma's cemetery.

When we came to dessert the waiter told us there was *zuppa di due colori*, and we really shouldn't miss the opportunity to have it; so we ordered small portions of this dessert, which really does seem to come straight from the land of milk and honey. it bears some resemblance to trifle, or to the Italian *zuppa inglese*, except that it is a far richer dish. Frau Meier-Neri, who comes from Reggio Emilia, later gave me the recipe in Zurich. Like most recipes from this region, it is far from simple, but it is worth the time and effort.

Zuppa di due colori
Parma trifle

Ingredients for 6:
For the sauce:
8 egg yolks
1 litre milk
8 tablespoons flour
3 tablespoons cocoa
1 vanilla pod
50 g butter
150 g sponge fingers
rum
Alchermes (red Tuscan herb liqueur) or another liqueur
100 g almonds
100 g plain chocolate
100 g candied fruit
250 ml whipping cream

*Beat the sugar and the egg yolks until light and fluffy.
Gradually add the flour and milk, together with the vanilla
pod, slit open, and bring almost to the boil, stirring constantly
on low heat. Remove from the heat and stir in the butter. Now
in another pan dissolve the cocoa in a little warm milk and
pour in half the sauce; bring it almost to the boil once more,
stirring constantly. Then allow the contents of both pans to cool
to room temperature, stirring them occasionally. Then pour the
fire-red Alchermes liqueur, distilled from herbs, on to one plate,
and the rum onto another; soak half the sponge fingers in each
plate.*

Shell the almonds after blanching them for a few moments. Then dry them out in a low oven until they have begun to take on colour. Chop with a knife. The chocolate should also be broken up and chopped. Cut the candied fruit up into small cubes.

When all these preparations are complete, cover the bottom of a bowl with sponge, soaked in each liqueur, sprinkle with the chocolate, the nuts and the fruit, and pour the vanilla sauce over the top. Next comes a second layer of sponge; sprinkle with more chocolate, almonds and candied fruit, and cover with the chocolate sauce. Leave in the fridge overnight, and serve dressed with whipped cream.

Ever since that first visit I have always enjoyed returning to Parma on my way to Tuscany or Rome, whether to admire Antelami's baptistry and the church domes painted by Correggio, or to buy Parmesan and *culatello*, because the Italians do not export the finest products of their food industry. There are hardly any cars in the centre of Parma, and its beautiful houses, its select shops and its elegantly dressed residents, men and women, create the effect of a salon where you are invited to linger. What's more, there are lots of splendid bars where both sweet and savory pastries are offered to the knowledgeable customers at almost any time of the day, freshly baked. Clients and staff have a lively, casual relationship; when a well-upholstered man at the counter mournfully announces that he is on a diet, the girl at the till will call out to suggest that in that case he had better go on a trip to another province.

No dish better expresses this delight in generous and imaginative eating than the macaroni pies that are still regarded in Emilia Romagna as the classic first course at special occasions. Only in these provinces, where the economy largely depends on the growing and processing of foodstuffs, would it occur to anyone to dress pasta with a rich sauce of meat, ham, sweetbreads, mushrooms and cheese and use it as the filling for a crusty pie. The famous cookery writer Pellegrino Artusi, mentioned earlier, begins his recipe for *pasticchio di maccheroni* with an anecdote about a man who was capable of wolfing down a twelve-man macaroni pastry; Artusi adds the nostalgic comment: "There are not so many of these greedy parasites as there once were. I think there are two reasons for this: the constitution of the human body has grown weaker, and there are intellectual pleasures, part of culture, that have taken the place of sensual ones."

It was in the restaurant "La Filoma" that I first ate a portion of a pasta pie, filled with spaghetti in a tomato and meat sauce, as well as melting mozzarella. Its particular appeal lies in the differing consistencies of the crusty shell and the soft-boiled pasta as well as in the contrast between the slightly sweet pastry and the aromatic, salty filling. I later discovered from Italian friends that pasta pies exist in several local traditions; Rosanna, who comes from Padua, cooked me one with macaroni and pigeon sauce, and Mariella introduced me to the Bologna version, the *pasticcio di tortellini*, which takes the idea of a generous filling to extremes by using tortellini, which themselves have a filling.

Mariella told me that her pasticcio is not nearly as much work as you might think, because instead of spending hours making the tortellini by hand, she buys "home-made" ones in an Italian shop and uses ready-rolled pastry. In place of the meat sauce of the classic recipe, she makes a béchamel sauce; she thinks this goes better with the meat-filled tortellini. I can confirm that the results of this unorthodox procedure of hers taste delicious.

Pasticcio di tortellini
Tortellini pie

400 g slightly sweet shortcrust pastry, or pre-rolled pastry
600 g tortellini, filled with meat
*béchamel sauce made with 30 g butter, 30 g flour, 300 ml milk, salt
    and grated nutmeg*

100 g boiled ham
150 g grated Parmesan
150 g mozzarella
50 g butter
1 egg yolk

Boil the tortellini in meat stock and allow to cool. Butter a springform and cover the base and sides with two-thirds of the rolled pastry. Then add a layer of tortellini followed by a few spoonsful of béchamel and some diced ham and mozzarella; sprinkle with Parmesan, dot with small pieces of butter, and continue adding layers in the same way till the pie is full. Cut a round lid out of the remaining pastry and place over the filling, pressing the edges together well. Apply the yolk to the lid with a pastry brush and make a few holes in it with a fork. Bake in a preheated oven at medium heat (200° C) for thirty to forty minutes.

Alberto Savinario's comment about Parmesan in his book about Milan hits the nail on the head: "Parmesan is a foundation cheese. What the double bass is to stringed instruments, Parmesan is to cheeses. The bottom note of Parmesan's deep, fatherly bass supports the lighter members of the cheese quartet, Taleggio and Crescenza, the violas and trebles of the family, the hoard of Robiolas and Stracchinos …" After a digression on Gruyère and Emmental he continues: "Parmesan is heavy, robust, reliable. Its special solid flavour is reflected in its shape, that of a waggon wheel. It is the 'giant Morgante' among cheeses. But Parmesan is not an only child; it has two brothers, *Reggiano* and *Lodigiano* – the three giants of the cheese world. The hieratic arrangement of this trinity of cheeses is striking – three serious brothers who have settled a short distance apart from each other on the same Roman road, running from north to south; each has a strong town as its base, like an army's garrison. Lodigiano is at home in Lodi, Reggiano in Reggio Emilia, and Parmesan in Parma." But since Savinio's book was published in 1944 the geographical disposition of north Italian cheeses has changed; in the name of industrialisation, Parmesan is made today in a legally defined zone of the provinces of Parma, Reggio Emilia and Modena on the right bank of the Po, and the bulk of the hard cheese produced in northern Italy carries the generic designation *Grana padano*.

Florence,
or white beans as an art form

It was one Easter that I first went on a trip to Florence, although I really prefer to spend public holidays at home. But this time I was happy to put up with all the inconveniences, because a friend had offered me the use of his flat in the centre of town, a stone's throw from the *Duomo*, for a week. I still clearly remember climbing up beautiful narrow stone steps all the way to the seventh floor with my suitcase before entering the enormous bare living room, with a fire burning in the grate and a spit turning. This friend welcomed me with a meal I shall never forget. It consisted of just grilled meat, unsalted country bread and pure, good Chianti.

Through this meal I gained an understanding of the art of Florentine cookery before making the acquaintance of the city; avoiding all elaboration, it concentrates on the essentials. To make a rather bold comparison, this strict simplicity recalls the perfection of an early Renaissance palazzo. Even tourists pressed for time cannot help noticing the contrast between the hearty, sumptuous cuisine of Emilia Romagna and the natural simplicity of Tuscan cooking. In Tuscany it is not imagination that triumphs, but the quality of natural produce, prepared without sophistication, but with the greatest care – starting with the unsalted country bread, made with rather coarse flour and with a hard crust and a firm crumb, so that it is tasty even when stale. The Chianti that is drunk in Florentine homes almost always comes straight from a trusted wine producer; it has a fresh and well-balanced flavour and never gives you a headache. Finally, in

71

Tuscan cooking there are no sauces to alter the flavour and disguise the outlines; the most popular method of cooking meat is to grill it or roast it on the spit. This includes the famous *bistecca fiorentina*, which is placed on the grill just as it comes from the butcher, about seven hundred grammes in weight, without being rubbed with oil or salt beforehand; the only important thing is for the charcoal to be hot but without flames; each side of the steak must be exposed to the effects of the heat for no more than 4–6 minutes. It goes without saying that the meat must be top quality.

In Tuscany, the olive oil must be first class too. Like wine, if possible it is bought straight from the producer rather than from a shop. The best oil comes from the province of Lucca, where sea and land breezes mix in the hills, making for a particularly delicious olive crop. The oil from Lucca is neither too rich nor too bitter, and it has a beautiful pale golden colour with a green shimmer. The first time I had it was in an osteria in Lucca; on the menu was written by hand *olio d'oliva di Buti*. The waiter informed me that Buti is a little village in the olive-growing hills of the surrounding area, and suggested I order some fennel *al pinzimonio* to try out this oil. Pinzimonio turned out to be a sauce of true Tuscan simplicity, and I think it is better than all the mousselines, Béarnaises and béchamels of French cookery; it consists simply of olive oil, freshly milled black pepper and a little salt. in this you dip raw fennel leaves, bits of celery, carrot sticks or the leaves of the delicate, violet green artichokes that grow in Sardinia and Liguria in the winter. The liking in Tuscany for eating raw vegetables has nothing to do with health food; it derives from the traditional poverty, which till the middle of the twentieth century forced the rural population of central and southern Italy to eke out their daily portion of bread with wild herbs and fruit.

Next to the grill, the spit is the most important piece of equipment in Florentine meat cookery, the mechanical turning spit in chimney breasts or ovens, used for baking *arista*, the rolled pork joint with rosemary, or a chicken bought, alive, from the market or from a farmer. In Tuscany as elsewhere, people also used to like roasting small birds on the spit. For the past six hundred years, roast fieldfares and thrushes have been among the favourite dishes of the citizens of Florence, as you can read in a short novella by Franco Sachetti which tells the story of how a clever woman defended her husband's wedding tackle from a starving cat's attack. Her text opens with a vivid portrayal of the man's total focus on his cooking: "One evening he had four splendid thrushes that he wanted to roast in his own way, and he had ordered his maid to put them by a fire that was burning in the hall. There he set up a roasting spit, sat on a stool and heaped up the embers, for he wanted the thrushes to be roasted according to all the rules of the art before enjoying them in well-earned peace with his wife."

These days, the environmentally-aware Florentines no longer eat thrushes, but kebabs have become very popular. They are called *uccelli scappati*, which translates literally as "flown away birds". They are made of veal, calves' liver, bacon and sage leaves, and the liver lends them something of the rather bitter gamey flavour of the little birds, which in Italy used to be part of the popular diet, just like snails, frogs and wild vegetables.

Uccelli Scappati
Veal skewers

200 g thin veal chops
200 g sliced calves' liver
200 g bacon
sage leaves
50 g butter
100–200 ml meat stock

Cut the meat, liver and bacon into approximately 4 cm squares. Put a piece of meat, a piece of liver, a piece of bacon and a sage leaf on a toothpick, repeating once for each toothpick; continue

73

till the ingredients are used up. Then melt the butter in a frying pan, add a sage leaf and fry the skewers well on all sides until they are a nice golden brown. Add a little stock, turn down very low and cook for about twenty minutes till done, adding a little more stock as needed.

Polenta goes very well with *uccelli scappati*. In Florence people eat white beans with them, as with almost all other meat dishes. It is these beans that are the favourite vegetable of the region, and not spinach as we assume when we use the term *alla fiorentina* to signify the addition of spinach; this was probably the invention of a French chef. In Tuscany, and indeed the whole of southern and central Italy, spinach is not very common at all, because it is a winter vegetable that bolts at high temperatures, producing only flowers and no more leaves. Instead of spinach *bieta* is grown, beet or chard, which has a coarser flavour but a longer season.

There is nothing the Florentines like more than white beans, and there is no city in Italy where they are more tastily cooked. Rather than boiling them carelessly in salted water that is then poured away, they make sure that they soak up their liquid gradually without losing any of their own flavour.

The curvaceous Chianti bottles gave the housewives of Florence the idea for a recipe called *al fiasco*; as well as being original, it is the gentlest and most delicate way of cooking white beans. *Fagioli al fiasco* are to be found on every menu in Florence. It is possible to make do without the soft glow of a charcoal fire and cook them like this in a moderately warm oven:

Fagioli al fiasco
Bottled white beans

300 g white beans
½ cup good olive oil
sage leaves
2 cloves of garlic
salt and pepper

Soak the beans overnight. The next day, remove the straw from a
Chianti bottle, wash the bottle thoroughly, and fill with the
soaked and drained beans. Add the oil, three cups water (¾ litre),
sage leaves and garlic. The bottle must not be more than ²/³ full;
seal it with a cork with a piece cut out of it to let the steam escape.
Cook the beans in the oven at low to medium heat (190° C) till
done, about 3½ hours. In the end, all the liquid must have been
soaked up by the beans. Put them in a dish and season with salt
and freshly-milled pepper. They may be served warm or cold.

Bean dishes do not always taste so good north of the Alps as they do in
Italy, and this may have something to do with the quality of the produce.
In Italy people eat a lot more pulses than in Switzerland, and the peas,
lentils and chickpeas in the markets are almost all from last year's harvest.
Just as we used to buy a supply of potatoes for the winter each autumn, in
Tuscany people buy enough beans for the whole year as soon as the new
harvest has been brought in. But in our shops older goods are often sold,
and even beans from different harvests that will not all be done in the
same amount of time. We have also forgotten that the fresh beans are a
real delicacy; in Tuscany and the rest of Italy a wealth of different kinds of
fagioli freschi appears on the menu in August and September.

The combination of pulses with pork, bacon or pork sausages are a classic more or less the world over. I was most impressed by the pork rind and vegetable stew, known as *fagioli al forno* in Florence, which I had in a simple *buca*, as the typical cellar restaurants on Florence are called, and so I asked the waiter for the recipe.

Fagioli al forno
Baked white beans

400 g dried white beans
300 g pork rind
2 cloves garlic
1 leek
1 tin peeled tomatoes
salt and pepper

Soak the beans overnight and put them, drained, in an ovenproof earthenware pot. Then wash the rind and cut into strips, crush the garlic, cut the leek into thin strips, and add to the beans, together with the tomatoes. Season and add enough water to cover the beans two fingers deep. Cover and cook for two and a half hours till done in a medium oven. The beans should be served in the pot without stirring them. The liquid should have been almost entirely soaked up by the beans.

There is one more famous Tuscan bean recipe called *fagioli all'uccelletto*, probably because the beans are seasoned with sage leaves, like the little birds on the spit. This method is quicker than the other two because the beans are boiled in salt water instead of being simmered till done in the oven. You can even use beans from a tin, preserved in salt water rather than tomato sauce. In this way white beans can become an excellent quick meal that will be ready in half an hour.

Fagioli all'uccelletto
White beans with sage

400 g dried white beans or
2 medium tins white beans, preserved in salt water
salt and pepper
6 tablespoons olive oil
2 cloves of garlic
fresh or dried sage leaves
2 medium tins peeled tomatoes

Soak the beans overnight in water and cook them in lightly-salted water till done; alternatively, open the tins and drain. Heat the oil and gently cook the garlic and sage a little. Then add the tomatoes and the drained beans, season and leave to cook through for about twenty minutes on low heat.

But the Tuscans are not just *mangiafagioli*, bean-eaters, as they are called in contrast to the *polentoni*, the north Italian polenta eaters. They also grow and eat a huge variety of vegetables: artichokes, broccoli, fennel, aubergines, green beans, peppers and celery, not to mention the incomparable delicate sweet peas, *piselli toscani*, that have nothing to do with the hard green balls that the deep-freeze industry serves up to us. It is an indicator of the different level of culinary civilization in north and south that this wonderful vegetable has practically disappeared from amongst our fresh produce, whereas in Italy it is on offer in spring in every local market and grocer. Fresh peas are not a time-consuming vegetable; they are soon cooked, and Italian housewives who have no time to prepare them can order a pound of shelled peas from their grocer.

There are two ways to cook fresh peas. The easiest method is to stew them in cold-pressed olive oil with chopped shallot or mild white onion, seasoning with salt and a pinch of sugar; serve as soon as they are done. The other method is called:

Piselli alla fiorentina
Peas alla fiorentina

1½ kg peas in the pod
100 ml olive oil
50 g pancetta (bacon)
1 clove of garlic
1 tablespoon chopped parsley
1 teaspoon sugar, salt

Prepare the peas and wash well. Put the finely-chopped garlic, the chopped pancetta and the oil into a pot and cook gently on a low heat till the garlic begins to turn yellow; then add the peas and parsley. If the peas are small and tender, they will be done within a few minutes; if they are more mature, add a little meat stock and boil till done. In either case they should be sprinkled with sugar before being removed from the heat.

The Good Bread of Tuscany

On the journey by motorway from the north to Rome, or vice versa, one hundred and eighty kilometres of Tuscany await you. Once on the plain after the many tunnels of the Appennine stretch, you soon reach the point when skirting Florence where the barrier between the two carriageways of the *autostrada del sole* is interrupted, opening up for a few moments an unimpeded view of Brunelleschi's splendid cathedral dome. To the south of the city begins the richly parcelled fertile hill landscape which induced Goethe, eager as he was to reach Rome, to make this remark in his *Italian Journey*: 'Everything here is at once industrious and pure; the aim is to combine utility with gracefulness. The fruitful care taken over everything is apparent.' From silver-grey olives and the various nuances of vineyards, orchards and market gardens to the night-black green of the dramatic cypresses, there is a striking palette of green tones.

The temptation to stop and get out is constant and compelling. That is how it was when I first went to Arezzo. Eva thought we should just be able to fit in a short visit to see Piero della Francesca's frescos. The motorway exit led us into a misty landscape, although Tuscany is supposed to be fog-free in winter. Nonetheless, the grey veiled countryside was truly charming; the mist also suited the town's painterly jumble of mediaeval alleys, interrupted by the occasional striking baroque palazzo. Then we stood before the bare, uncompleted façade of San Francesco; between 1453 and 1464, Piero della Francesca decorated its main chapel with the frescos of the legend of the True Cross. The church was shut, which at half past four is unheard of. When we asked at the kiosk on the corner, the friendly woman had no idea where the guard, the warden, or the priest might be. She advised us to go and see the cathedral or the Pieve di Santa Maria, which she said were also nice churches. We took this advice, and afterwards had a cappuccino to warm ourselves up in a bar on the crooked, sloping *piazza grande*.

At twenty past five we were back in front of San Francesco; the door remained firmly shut. But we did not give in to this Italian unreliability. We found ourselves a hotel room and had a talk with the concierge about the local restaurants, which induced us to make the pilgrimage to San Francesco for a third time, where we were at least able to have a decent meal in the 'Buca di San Francesco'. The *pappardelle sulla lepre* (pasta with hare sauce), an Arezzan speciality and also the only well-known Tuscan noodle dish, would have been enough on its own to make it worth our while. A rich dish combining the first course of pasta or soup with the meat course, it is a meal in itself. The Tuscans are passionate hunters who prefer game to all other meat; they eat their beloved noodles with boar or game stew as well as hare. Since the sixties and seventies though, hunting has become a pastime of such unbridled popularity that there would be neither wild boar nor pheasant in Tuscany today if they were not specially bred and released just before the opening of the season. Stricter hunting laws have been under discussion for years, but without any result. Here is a recipe with rabbit, which may be cooked throughout the year.

Pappardelle col coniglio
Pasta with rabbit stew

500 g pasta
1 rabbit
1 bottle Chianti

1 onion
1 piece of celery
peppercorns
thyme
1 bay leaf
100 g butter
pinch nutmeg
salt and pepper
1 tablespoon flour
200 ml cream

Have the rabbit cut up into stewing pieces and place them overnight in a dish with the chopped onion, the celery and the spices, covered with the wine. The next day drain the marinade off, reserving, together with the onion and celery. Pat the meat dry with kitchen paper and fry until nicely golden brown in 30 g butter. Season with salt and pepper, and gradually pour in the marinade, including the vegetables, then leave to simmer in a well-covered casserole till done, for about two hours. Now put the stew in a sieve, reserving the juices. Melt 30 g butter in a frying pan and fry the flour in it; add the sieved juices, followed by the cream, and allow to simmer on low heat for a quarter of an hour, season with salt and pepper and a pinch of nutmeg. Meanwhile, separate the tender meat from its bones and return the pieces to the sauce. Boil the pasta till al dente, drain and combine in a hot bowl with 30 g butter pieces and a little of the rabbit sauce. Bring the pasta and the sauce to the table separately, putting pasta on each plate first and then a spoonful of sauce on top.

The recipe for this pasta dish is one of Beatrice's; she has thought up a good starter to go with it. She cuts the rabbit liver into thin slices, which she quickly fries in butter, serving them with rocket.

As well as this recipe, I am also grateful to Beatrice for a holiday I spent in her flat in Castagneto-Carducci, which is a small town between the Tuscan hills and the coast of the Tyrrhenian Sea. It was a hot August and the town was overflowing with tourists, the beach was packed, and rubbish was scattered through the pine forest. Yet when at night a sea breeze cooled off the spectators in the open-air cinema, the full moon would outshine the big screen. In the daytime Lorenzo and I went on trips to the hinterland, a wild untouched landscape of *macchia* (scrub), oak and chestnut woods, tumbledown farmyards and isolated villages. It was on these outings that we got to know the country cooking of Tuscany, which is quite different from Florentine cuisine. In the villages people do not eat steaks and roasts; the expensive beef is sold to the town-dwellers, but instead they make wonderful minestrone, eaten cold in summer, and excellent bean soup. *Ribollita* was a find, a bean soup served like French onion soup, with slices of bread sprinkled with grated Parmesan and grilled in the oven.

In the Tuscan diet, bread takes the place of pasta – the unsalted country bread that tastes so good, they will eat it with a glass of wine without any other accompaniment, though they tend to sprinkle it with a little salt. The housewife uses a lot of bread for cooking too, and one of the best bread dishes we ate was in a rosticceria in Volterra where Lorenzo ordered a roast chicken, and the owner suggested we try some *panzanella* as a starter. He brought us a brown terracotta dish containing a cool white sauce mixed with pieces of tomato and cucumber and chopped basil leaves.

Panzanella
Bread salad

6 slices good country bread
2 tomatoes

1 large onion
½ cucumber
basil leaves
2 tablespoons vinegar
4 tablespoons olive oil
salt and pepper

Cut the crust off the bread and soak in cold water until it is soft enough to be crushed with a fork. Then finely chop the onions, cut the tomatoes and the cucumber into small pieces, and mix in with the bread. Make a salad dressing from the vinegar, oil, chopped basil leaves and the salt and pepper; stir this in. Put the finished dish in the fridge for an hour or so before eating.

This panzanarella *is really nothing more than a simple variation of the Spanish gazpacho; in the Tuscan countryside it is regarded as a meal in itself, containing all the necessities of life, from the vitamins to the oil. What's more, the ingredients are to hand throughout the summer in every home. A spoonful of capers may be added as an embellishment. Those who like a bit of heat can sprinkle the salad with finely grated or chopped chillies when it is ready to serve.*

If you acquire a taste for this peasant starter, you will never have a problem using up stale bread again. Our young neighbour in Castagneto gave me the recipe for another excellent bread dish; on her day off she used to cook a big pot of *pappa col pomodoro*, a tasty soup made of tomatoes, garlic, basil, olive oil and old bread, just as good eaten warm or cold. Since garlic is regarded in Tuscany and in large parts of Italy as a cure for worms, this soup often used to be given to children, especially when weaning. That is probably the origin of the name *pappa*, purée. There is also a famous old hit whose refrain, "La pa-pa-pa, La pa-pa-pa, col po- mo- do- ro", can still be heard issuing from juke boxes in Italian bars.

Pappa col pomodoro
Tomato soup

1 kg ripe tomatoes (or 2 tins peeled tomatoes)
350 g stale country bread
200 ml olive oil
1½ litres meat stock
6 cloves of garlic
plenty of basil leaves
salt and pepper

*Quarter the tomatoes and cook on moderate heat till soft; then
sieve them, or put them through the mouli. Cut the stale bread
into slices and toast them well in the oven. Then warm up the
stock, which should not be too strongly flavoured, and add the
sieved tomatoes, the bread, the oil, the chopped garlic and the
coarsely-chopped basil leaves, and season; leave to cook on low
heat until the liquid has all but evaporated and the soup has
become a thick sauce. Pour into soup bowls with a little olive oil
of the best quality.* Pappa col pomodoro *also tastes good
warmed up.*

But in Tuscan cookery plenty of use is made of fresh bread too. One of
the simplest and best starters is *bruschetta*, the name in Tuscany and the
Abruzzi for toast rubbed with garlic, drizzled with olive oil and sprinkled
with salt and pepper. In many trattorias in Tuscany and southern Italy, a
piece of bruschetta is automatically served with the wine, warm from the
oven. If the oil and the bread are of good quality, this peasant snack tastes
better than smoked salmon. Another version is tomato bread, familiar
all the way from Tuscany to Calabria: a piece of dry bread rubbed with

a clove of garlic and topped with half a tomato; the bread soaks up its juice. Then olive oil is poured over it, and salt and pepper added to taste. In Tuscany, *crostini* are also popular, little toasted pieces of bread with various toppings. In the autumn they are usually served with game stew. A delicacy to be had all year round are *crostini di fegatini di pollo*, with chicken liver; they are mostly served warm as a starter, but they go well cold too with a glass of Chianti.

Crostini di fegatini
Chicken liver crostini

8 slices country bread
8 chicken livers
1 onion
2 anchovies
2 tablespoons of butter
sage leaves
½ tablespoon of tomato purée
2 tablespoons of capers
½ glass wine
salt and pepper
1 tablespoon grated Parmesan
butter for the tin

Chop the onion and the anchovies and allow to take colour in the butter; add the livers and the sage leaves and fry a little longer. Then remove the livers from the pan and chop very finely. Add the tomato purée, the finely-chopped capers and the wine to the butter, allow to warm through, and then combine the liver with the sauce and the cheese. Season to taste and spread the liver paste on the slices of bread, cut in two. Place on a tin greased with butter and grill in a preheated oven on high for five minutes.

NB The slightly superior and more delicate flavour of crostini in Tuscany in comparison with ones made according to this recipe does not derive from the local atmosphere. Tuscan housewives and cooks spread the chicken livers with 50% melts. This secret is not mentioned in the presence of tourists.

We only went on the beach at Donoratico in the evening, when the sun was already on the point of setting and the beach attendants had already cleaned up the sand for the next day. In the relatively cool evening air, the sea was as warm as the water in a bath. On the way home we went past Marzio's a few times, a modern fish restaurant where you could eat the best seafood salad, black cuttlefish risotto, grilled fish, and the famous Livorno fish soup, called *cacciuco*.

I took a very simple starter away from this restaurant; it is also known in Liguria, indeed probably on all Mediterranean coasts.

Acciughe al limone
Anchovies in lemon juice

The key to this dish is very fresh anchovies; gut them, remove the heads and backbones, open up and lay next to each other on a platter. Pour plenty of lemon juice over them and leave for 24 hours in the fridge. During this time the raw fish "cooks in the lemon juice", as they say in Italy, and is ready to eat. They may also be seasoned with a little salt and good olive oil or a mixture of finely chopped garlic and parsley. I like them best "neat", because I find the combination of fish fresh from the sea with lemon juice more subtle.

In country inns in Tuscany, you will often be offered a glass of *vinsanto* at the end of a meal, a golden yellow medium-dry dessert wine that is fermented from sun-dried grapes throughout Tuscany and stored in barrels for at least three years. It is served with dry almond biscuits, which are called *cantucci, giottini* or *biscottini di Prato* depending on the area. This pleasantly brittle dessert reflects the stern and thrifty nature of Tuscan cuisine, and in a sense that of all Italy, where desserts were never that important, perhaps because fresh, sweet fruit is available here all year round to finish off a meal after the cheese. This theory can be tested out on Italian cookbooks, where the desserts and cakes take up at most a tenth of the total space, whereas a third of all the recipes in a German cookbook are devoted to this theme. So to end this chapter, here is the recipe for:

Cantucci
Tuscan almond biscuits

500 g flour
500 g sugar
250 g almonds
1 pinch baking powder
4 eggs
salt
butter and flour to grease and dust the tin

Blanch the almonds and shell them, drying them for ten minutes in the oven before chopping them up with a knife. Stir the flour, sugar, eggs and baking powder together to make the biscuit mixture, then gradually add the almonds to it. It will need thorough kneading. Shape into little rolls and place on the buttered and floured tin; bake in a medium oven (150° C) for 7–8 minutes. Then take the rolls out and slice across into slices about 1 cm thick. Return the tin to the oven and bake a further ten minutes till done. The cantucci will stay fresh for several months in a biscuit tin.

Umbria,
or the true nature of Ricotta

I will never forget the car park in front of the Basilica of St Francis in Assisi. It ought to be a fine broad square, surrounded on three sides by fifteenth-century colonnades, but all the cars with plates from far-flung countries, the parking attendants, the multilingual guides and the innumerable pilgrims are a confusing distraction. I was parking a friend's car, and because I wasn't used to its size, I managed to dent it. I ended up having words with a French woman even though her Peugeot hadn't received so much as a scratch in the process. The thing that annoyed me was that it was my friend's car that had been damaged – he was attending a conference in Perugia that evening. And so I strolled grumpily through the mediaeval town; I thought it was far too well-kept and there were too many decorative red geraniums. I bought a hand-embroidered handker-chief in a souvenir shop and discovered that the famous Assisi embroidery had been being made in Apulia for decades.

Around eight, I had dinner in a restaurant with Umbrian cooking called "La Stalla", recommended to me by the concierge. The waiter gave me a seat at a long wooden table where other customers were already sitting. The lentil soup with rice that I discovered on the menu had run out, and so I decided on bean soup with pasta. It was served hot, steaming and sprinkled with fresh parsley in a brown glazed earthenware bowl, and my neighbour, a coach driver for pilgrims, was eating polenta with lamb stew. He said reflectively that nothing was better than a dish of *pasta e fagioli*.

Talking to this neighbour, and to a couple from Lecce who were sitting opposite, I realized that the Italian national dish is not pasta or pizza, but *pasta e fagioli*, the bean soup with pasta that is known and loved from the Veneto to Calabria. It is a dish of Franciscan simplicity, wholesome, cheap and decidedly healthy. Nutritionists too confirm this when they recommend pulses as a source of vitamins, minerals and protein, suggesting they be eaten with foods rich in carbohydrate, because they are taken up particularly well by the body in this combination. If you ask an Italian which pulses he likes eating best, the answer depends on his geographical origins: those from the south will say *ceci* (chickpeas), those from central Italy *toscanelli* (white beans) and northerners *borlotti* (red and white speckled beans).

The way the bean soup is combined with pasta also varies from region to region; in southern and central Italy, lentils and *fave* (broad beans) are commonly used as well as chickpeas, and the starchy pasta may be replaced by rice, barley or maize. These nutritious dishes are a demonstration of the cookery of the poor; though its first aim must be to satisfy hunger, it is imaginative too. The range of possible combinations becomes almost unlimited once you discover that these soups also taste good with tomatoes and wild vegetables, and that they can be made with mussels, prawns and fish as well as bacon and ham. Here is a classic recipe that can be made with white beans or borlotti beans. If the beans are freshly picked, at least double the quantity will be needed, but they will not need soaking.

Pasta e fagioli
Bean soup with pasta

200 g dried beans
2 tablespoons oil
1 onion
1 pinch of cinnamon

salt and pepper
2–3 soup bones
50 g bacon
200 g pasta, or soup pasta (tiny pasta shapes)
50 g Parmesan
chopped parsley

Soak the beans overnight and bring to the boil in fresh cold water, together with the oil, the chopped onion, the soup bones, the finely-chopped bacon, salt, pepper and cinnamon. Once they have come to the boil, allow to simmer covered for 2–3 hours on very low heat, until the beans are almost disintegrating. Then break the pasta into pieces and boil till al dente. *Sprinkle the parsley on to the soup and serve with freshly grated Parmesan. The pecorino served with this soup in central and southern Italy gives it a powerful country flavour.*

Everyone who knows Italy knows that Orvieto is one of the most beautiful towns in Umbria. Between Florence and Rome, a great lump of rock suddenly rises up out of the gently rolling plain, a massive tuffstone outcrop on which the tightly-packed town stands with its Gothic cathedral, one of the most splendid churches in Italy. About twenty years ago Luigi Malerba bought the bishop's summer villa, ten kilometres to the south of Orvieto – the bishop needed the money to build an ugly modern church. The country around Orvieto has a sad reputation as a museum of postmodern Italian architectural horrors; between olive groves and vineyards, holm oaks and ruined monasteries, appalling mushroom-shaped buildings can be found with enormous pointy roofs that extend far beyond the area of the ground floor, with huge dormer windows on all sides. This is a cheap ploy to get round the planning regulations, which stipulate that new buildings in this area should only have one storey; and it is the doing of the Romans, who build their weekend villas in this lovely region, an hour's drive from the capital.

Malerba's former Episcopal summer house at Settecamini is a simple square building, three hundred years old and so splendidly proportioned that you almost feel lost in the big rooms. Nearby is a chestnut wood with an unopened Etruscan burial mound, and hens, guinea fowl, ducks and sheep wander by the farmhouse. This is where I first became acquainted with Italian country life, starting with my discovery of ricotta, a milk product that our modern dairy industry has lost sight of. It is a component of the whey, the watery greenish liquid created during the making of cheese. It contains hardly any fat, but is a valuable source of protein. It used to be used to feed pigs, or to make cheese by heating it until a light white substance formed in clumps: whey cheese or ricotta. Today it is exported as a product of the Italian dairy industry in plastic pots, unfortunately with added cream and stabilizers. Its flavour is agreeably reminiscent of fresh milk, and after Parmesan and mozzarella it is the most important dairy product in Italian cooking. Ricotta is always regarded as equivalent to curd cheese, but that is the relatively rich and slightly soured fresh cheese, which is made when the milk is curdled with rennet. Perhaps it can be used in some recipes as a substitute for ricotta, but the taste, consistency and nutritional value of the two products are quite different. One mild, sunny March morning I was sitting in the kitchen with my espresso when Anna Malerba came in and put a wooden tray on the table. Three beautifully woven little reed baskets stood on it, covered with white cloths. I asked her where she had got these attractive baskets, but she said I ought to be more interested in where the contents came from. It was fresh sheep's milk ricotta that she had just bought from the farmer's wife. It was still lukewarm and possessed an exquisite fresh flavour. Reed baskets are the traditional containers the ricotta is put in to drain, and they imprint their delicate ornamental pattern on the ricotta when it is ready. The fresh, snow-white mound seemed to convey the essence of a peasant culture that we have lost. What use are all the delicacies of the world when we no longer know the taste of fresh, warm whey cheese in reed baskets!

For lunch, Anna made a sort of gnocchi or dumplings out of the fresh ricotta. In Umbria they are called *malfatti*, or 'badly made', because the dumplings, shaped with a pair of teaspoons, turn out rather irregularly. They are a wonderful starter, seasoned with fresh butter and grated Parmesan – a harmonious trio of Italian dairy products.

Malfatti
Ricotta dumplings

300 g ricotta
80 g flour
salt, nutmeg
100 g grated Parmesan
2 eggs
2 egg yolks
to serve:
50 g fresh butter
50 g grated Parmesan

Beat the eggs and the yolks well and mix in the ricotta, stirring vigorously. Then fold in the flour and the Parmesan, seasoning with salt and nutmeg. Leave to stand for half an hour, then form small balls with two teaspoons and place on a floured board or a plate. To test whether the consistency is right, cook a test dumpling in a small pan of boiling water. Then bring a large pan of unsalted water to the boil and cook the dumplings in it till done, about three minutes. Remove with a slotted spoon and dress them with the Parmesan and the butter, cut into little pieces.

Ricotta is suited to both sweet and savoury dishes. Seasoned with salt and pepper and beaten till smooth with a little cooking water, it makes an easy and quickly prepared spaghetti sauce. If mixed with sweetened coffee and chilled, it becomes a mocha dessert that has hardly any calories.

But the finest ricotta dessert must be Anna Malerba's *torta di ricotta*, similar to cheesecake. It is not that easy to make, but it is worth following the recipe below step by step; made properly, this is a cake of pure and wholesome flavour with a half crunchy, half melting consistency.

Torta di ricotta
Ricotta cake

Ingredients for eight:
For the pastry:
150 g flour
50 g potato flour (or Maizena)
100 g sugar
100 g butter
1 egg
a pinch of cinnamon
For the filling:
250 g sugar
30 g flour
2 eggs
500 ml milk
300 g ricotta
1 egg yolk
grated lemon zest

To make the pastry, form a mound of the two flours and put the sugar, the butter (at room temperature) and the cinnamon in the middle. Knead together to form a ball. Butter a springform well, place the ball in the middle and press out with your fingers until the base and sides of the tin are entirely covered.

For the filling, first beat the eggs with 150 g sugar in a pan on medium heat until fluffy; then gradually stir in the heated milk in small amounts. Cook the liquid for about ten minutes, stirring constantly; allow to cool, stirring occasionally to stop a skin forming. When it has cooled, pour the liquid into a large bowl, add the ricotta, 100 g sugar and the egg yolk; mix, stirring well. Put on top of the pastry in the tin and bake for about 45 minutes at 190–200 degrees C in a preheated oven. Allow to cool and put in the fridge an hour before eating.

Anna Malerba also taught me that milk and butter can be used to cook roast veal with hardly any work; the dish has a tender and refined flavour.

Arrosto di vitello al latte
Braised veal with milk

1 kg loin or fillet of veal
50 g butter
1 litre milk

Melt the butter in a casserole and fry the meat, that you have rubbed with salt and pepper, very slowly all over on low heat. Then gradually add the milk, and leave to braise on very low heat for one and a half to two hours till done. Slice the meat, place it on a heated platter and keep warm. reduce the sauce until it becomes thick and lumpy; now pass through a sieve or purée with a hand blender. Pour a third of the sauce over the sliced joint, serving the rest separately.

This is the only meat dish I know that requires absolutely no seasoning – not even salt. At any rate, Anna Malerba doesn't put any salt in; as far as she is concerned, a litre of milk contains quite enough salt to season the dish. I am a bit less of a purist, so I rub the meat with a little salt and pepper before browning it.

Together with the tenant farmer's family, Anna and Luigi Malerba take care of the cultivation of the estate, the vines and olives, the potatoes and wheat, the vegetables and the pets. I saw how they talked new planting systems over with the farmers, and they both managed to combine a respect for country traditions with total rejection of anything that might harm the environment. Anna, who studies literature at the University of Rome and has a good knowledge of contemporary Italian literature, also knows all about distilling grappa and making sausages; she makes sure her thin black pigs only get healthy things like chestnuts, maize and acorns to eat. Hams, bacon and salami hang from the roof of her larder, and the shelves are full of bottles of home-bottled tomato sauce.

The Malerbas have salad with every meal, lunch and dinner – the sort of mixed green salad that is popular throughout central and southern Italy. It contains at least three kinds of lettuce, usually *radicchio*, *endivia* and *lattuga*. Then there are aromatic herbs; if possible there should be some *rughetta*, dark green and intensely bitter, and Anna picks whatever is to be had at the time of year in the meadow, a variety of watercress called *zampa di gallo*, or *pimpinella*, pimpernel. Rughetta resembles the famous hemlock that Socrates was poisoned with, though, which grows in large quantities around Orvieto, and it is with a shudder that the Malerbas remember the hemlock salad they once served their guests years before – fortunately the guests knew enough botany to spot the mistake.

The flavour of this mixed green salad is so rich and harmonious that the salads served in Italian restaurants outside Italy, mixed with tomatoes, cucumber and fennel, seem fairly barbaric in comparison. It should be dressed with salt, olive oil and wine vinegar. Anna makes her own wine vinegar, and she has a *mamma* – vinegar starter culture – that she throws away every spring, rather than simply giving it a good wash as I do, reserving just a little bit which then soon regenerates in the vinegar wine. Another thing I learned from her is that the vinegar should not be left in the bottle with the starter for too long, or it will get too sour. Anna drains it off into 700 ml bottles, putting a peeled clove of garlic in each one, just enough to add an almost imperceptible hint of garlic to the salad.

Rome: old ruins and fresh vegetables

I am not sure which season in Rome is the nicest – the hot summer when all the Romans are at the sea and the city centre is like a peaceful village, or the brilliant autumn with its intense colours, or the mild winter, or the changeable spring. But all gourmets agree that spring is the best time of year when it comes to Roman cooking. There is tender lamb, scented herbs, and most of all there are fresh vegetables; these play a far more important rôle in the cooking of the Italian capital than we generally tend to think.

There are almost as many markets in Rome as there are classical ruins; Roman housewives buy their vegetables fresh every day in a local market or at one of the two large markets held in the Campo dei Fiori and the Piazza Vittorio Emmanuele near the railway station. You cannot truly know Rome without having experienced the colourful beauty of one of its markets and admiring the artichokes, peas, beans, broccoli, green asparagus, oyster mushrooms and the purple aubergines piled up on each stall with care and elegance in a decorative arrangement, and seeing the baskets of many different kinds of lettuce and asking the stall holder to make you up a mixed green salad consisting of tasty little leaves of all shades of green, rounded off with wild herbs. It is a pleasure to watch the market people, who use every free minute to shell peas or beans, clean vegetables for minestrone, or cut up white *puntarelle* (a variety of chicory) to form rings in cold water. People in Rome are so fond of vegetables that

99

they think of them as a dish in themselves, and often even as a substitute for meat or fish. Throughout southern Italy, the finest spaghetti sauces are made with artichokes, broccoli, aubergines, mushrooms and courgettes rather than with tomatoes.

For me, the best vegetarian pasta dish of all is the little pasta shells with broccoli, which I first ate with Laura Giuliani. You eat them with a lively oil, garlic and anchovy sauce that gets right inside the mussel-shaped pasta. Rather than tinned anchovies preserved in oil, Laura always uses salted ones, which have a wonderfully intense flavour of the sea. You need to open them up, remove the backbone and then rinse off the salt crystals under the tap. (Capers too have a far more powerful flavour if they are preserved in salt rather than vinegar.)

Conchiglie e broccoli
Pasta shells with broccoli

500 g pasta shells
500 g broccoli
1 glass olive oil
2 cloves of garlic
a crushed peperoncino (red chilli)
2 salted anchovies

Divide the broccoli into florets and put in boiling water with the pasta; they will be done in ten minutes or so. Meanwhile, heat the oil in a pan, add the finely-chopped garlic, the peperoncino and the anchovies, crushing them with a fork until they break up. Combine the drained shells and the broccoli with the sauce, serving without grated cheese.

   This combination of pasta, vegetables and a little bit of fish is healthy and nutritious enough to provide a light meal in itself, as well as being quick to prepare. Cauliflower may be used instead of broccoli. A friend I once cooked these cauliflower shells with thought the juxtaposition of similar colours was most effective.

It was the Giulianis too who introduced me to courgette or pumpkin flowers stuffed with mozzarella and anchovies. I remembered these delicate yellow cup-shaped flowers in their unfilled form from my student days in Naples, where they could be bought in all the markets in early summer. In those days you could buy them from street vendors who tossed them in a pot of seething oil before fishing them out with a slotted spoon and laying them on a piece of greaseproof paper which they then folded neatly into a bag, handing it over ceremoniously like a present. The filled Roman kind is substantial enough to be eaten as a light main course with a salad.

Fritto di fiori di zucca
Deep-fried pumpkin or marrow flowers

12 pumpkin flowers
100 g flour
250 ml white wine
white of an egg
100 g mozzarella
12 anchovy fillets (6 salted anchovies)
oil for deep frying

Wash the flowers and place on kitchen paper to dry. Place the flour and salt in a bowl and add the wine and olive oil. Mix

101

well with a whisk or an electric beater before folding in the egg white, beaten till stiff. Put a piece of cheese and an anchovy fillet inside each flower. Dip the flowers in the batter and immerse them in the boiling oil and allow to fry till golden brown on all sides, moving around freely in the oil. Remove with a slotted spoon, drain on kitchen paper and serve hot.

Strips of Parma ham may be used instead of anchovy fillets.

The importance of exquisitely cooked vegetables in Roman family cooking was brought home to me one evening at the Malerbas' house near the Piazza Navona when Francesco Sanvitale and Fabio Carpi as well as Alberto Moravia had been invited to dinner. The discussion took off over the starter, *carciofi alla romana*, tender young spring artichokes – they are very tasty, braised in oil with a spicy herb mixture between the leaves. We complimented the cook, but she insisted that it was at Alberto Moravia's that she had had the best artichokes she had ever eaten, a kind of crispy gratin. The novelist disagreed in embarrassed and curmudgeonly tones, maintaining that the only artichokes he liked apart from Anna Malerba's *carciofi alla romana* were *carciofi alla giuda*, Jewish artichokes; the conversation then turned to a consideration of the authentic recipe for this old dish from the Roman ghetto, where the artichokes are deep-fried in hot oil and pressed flat in the process so that they eventually resemble golden brown chrysanthemums.

Here is Anna Malerba's recipe for

Carciofi alla romana
Artichokes alla romana

8 small artichokes
1 lemon

parsley
2 cloves of garlic
fresh mint
salt, pepper, olive oil

For this dish to be successful, the best quality artichokes are essential, young and tender. It is also important to prepare them ruthlessly and without false economy, cutting off all hard or dry parts. Trim them with a sharp knife, leaving a stem just three or four centimetres long; remove the bottom layer of the base as well. Pluck off the outermost leaves and remove the points whilst slowly turning the artichoke in your left hand. Then open it up a little so you can remove the choke with a small spoon. Afterwards place in cold water, acidulated with lemon juice. Chop the parsley, mint and garlic and press this herb filling in between the leaves of the artichoke. Rub with salt and pepper before placing with the stalk facing upwards in a casserole containing plenty of heated olive oil. Add enough water to half cover the artichokes. Put on the lid and simmer for 20–50 minutes till done. By this time, the cooking liquid should have entirely evaporated. These artichokes taste just as good warm or cold. The herb filling may be combined with a few finely-chopped anchovy fillets or with anchovy paste.

To get to a good meal in Rome, there is no need to own the Guide Michelin or the Guida dell'Espresso; just ask for the address of a good trattoria in a bar, a newspaper kiosk, or in a tobacconists. If this is not possible, you can just leave things to chance and choose a place, which is busy at lunch or dinner time. It goes without saying that restaurants with special tourist menus are to be avoided. It is indispensable to know the language, because Italian waiters are keen to advise their clients and accommodate all their special requests with a smile, but only when you can explain as precisely as possible what you would like to eat do you become a valued and carefully served guest. So instead of simply ordering the vegetables that are listed on the menu, you should give an indication for the benefit of the chef as to how they are to be cooked – with oil or butter, with onions or garlic, hot or cold, with *peperoncino* or with a little fresh lemon juice.

Giorgio Manganelli is a master of culinary communication with waiters, and he often meets friends in the evenings at one of the four restaurants in the capital that meet his strict requirements. His fame as a writer and especially as a columnist on the front page of the Roman daily *Il Messaggero* does lend his gastrosophical presence special weight, but he still gives his full attention to educating waiters and chefs every time. This means that he turns up at the restaurant early in Roman terms, at eight o'clock, when the waiters have time for individual service and can go into any special requests with due respect. In the 'Bersagliere' by the Porta Pia he also always picks a table in the basement, where other customers will not appear until the ground floor section gets too crowded later on in the evening. He need no more than glance at the *abbacchio arrosto* to confirm sadly that the spring lamb was left ten minutes too long in the oven and so can no longer be as juicy as it ought to be; while eating a wild pigeon he may suddenly put his knife and fork resignedly down on his plate and tell the waiter rushing past that the bird is tough. After a brief consultation he allows himself to be persuaded to try a guinea fowl that is guaranteed to be tender.

Far from being in any way embarrassing, these ritualized exchanges are part of the varied and exciting experience of supper in a restaurant, an experience acted out by the writer, together with the waiters, the owner and the other customers in subsidiary roles. More than anyone, the waiters take part with gusto, acting in turn worried, shocked, concerned, relieved, warm and thankful, before finally accompanying the honoured *Professore* out on to the street where the taxi they ordered for him will already be waiting.

Once I also went to a supper at the house of a friend of Manganelli's; the tone of the meal was clearly influenced by the writer's baroque style. It began with a rich and colourful selection of southern Italian antipasti:

sweet tomatoes from Apulia bottled in oil and flavoured with oregano, wild green asparagus, black olives with a hint of orange scent, sweet and braised onions, shiny brown mushrooms and all different kinds of bright red spicy sausages seasoned with paprika. Then we had a *risotto nero*, rice dyed black with cuttlefish juice, which looks macabre at first sight, but tastes wonderfully of the sea; then a crispy baked duck, richly stuffed, served with potatoes sautéed with onions. The grand finale was an extravagant *gelato di formaggio*, made by our hostess according to Manganelli's instructions from a blended mixture of equal parts of Gorgonzola, Roquefort and whipped cream, and frozen. A different wine was served with each course, and a fine old port with the cheese ice cream. To round off the meal, a large bowl of refreshing kumquats, little Chinese mandarins, was brought to the table; with delicate precision, Manganelli called them *mandarini da camera*, because they were to be compared to ordinary mandarins as chamber music is to orchestral music.

It is no surprise that Manganelli is also very knowledgeable about the specific psychological effects of certain foods, or of eating them in a certain order; his essay 'In praise of eating' contains an interesting discussion of this topic. 'I know of no cure for anxiety as good as the *peperoncino*; quivering and biting, it will turn your ragged clothes into an immaculate jacket with a flower in the buttonhole. Tender, uncertain souls become almost cheeky after just a simple, slightly vulgar dish of spaghetti generously seasoned with *peperoncino*. A mixed casserole with sweet-sour fruits in mustard sauce seeds from Cremona engenders the calm outlook of maturity and the feeling a father has when all his many children are well established in life. A Wiener Schnitzel can only have the right effect if it is placed in the right context: in the middle of the week, it creates calm relaxation and the conviction that the end of the world won't affect us. An omelette may move us to tears, while at the same time it can communicate enough childish warmth and tender comfort to enable us to sail round the cape of a stormy night of the cruelest solitude. Murderous inclinations may be suppressed by rough, tasty dishes like ham bones and the divine pork rind with white or brown beans; the latter can also distract us from suicidal thoughts, though more flattering refinements of flavour may be still better suited to this task, such as delectable game seasoned with elegant impulsiveness. All those in low spirits should be served red wine, but white wine is best for the superstitious, the possessed, and dark spirits. It is no accident that vampires fear garlic, and anyone with a taste for it possesses a chthonic amulet, a mandrake from the heart of the earth to drive out the dark shadows of his innermost troubles. The onion is cunning, lusty and bold; the radish is full of pride, the leek is sublime, and they all are just the thing for brains which may be inspired to write poetry.'

The Abruzzi,
or the mystery of the pepper pod

There may not be many lovers of Italy who have experienced the Abruzzi as a skiing paradise, as I did – with deep blue sky, warm January sunshine and a shining white mountain setting. This was during the year I spent studying in Naples; in January and February we met on Sunday mornings at seven in the Piazza Garibaldi, which was dark and deserted, got on a bus, and dozed off again. Three hours later, we were in snowbound Roccaraso at a height of 1200 metres, surrounded by ski lifts. For a few hours we enjoyed dashing about on the pistes, stopping only for a cappuccino or an espresso; at around three in the afternoon we gathered in the trattoria for a meal that was lunch and dinner rolled into one.

These were cheery, sumptuous meals, where I made the acquaintance of the confusing variety of ways of cooking spaghetti, in refreshing contrast to the monotony of spaghetti in tomato sauce, which we lived off in Naples. But the greatest discovery was the pure heat of the *peperoncino*, the red chilli pepper that predominates in the cooking of this mountain province.

I still remember the famous *maccheroni alla chitarra* well, made by passing a thin pasta dough through a guitar-like contraption with stretched-out wires. They were very light and delicate, and were served with tomato sauce. After the first forkful I felt as though I had swallowed fire; my friends from Naples laughed when I reached for my water glass to put out the fire in my throat, and pointed out the strings of dried pepper pods decorating the walls of the restaurant. In the Abruzzi people like their food hot, and there are hardly any savoury dishes that are not generously seasoned with these incredibly hot red pods. It's hardly surprising they are called *diavoletti*, or little devils. But it is one of the mysteries of gastronomy why the oil that is spiced with these diabolical pods is called *olio santo*, or holy oil, blending the satanic and the sacred. This hot oil is used for browning meat, for vegetables and even for salad dressing.

Spaghetti con aglio, olio e peperoncino is also an authentically Abruzzan dish. This spaghetti sauce, made from garlic, oil and chillies, has been one of my favourite dishes ever since our skiing trips to Roccaraso; the ingredients can be kept permanently to hand, and it only takes a minute to make.

Spaghetti con aglio, olio e peperoncino
Spaghetti with garlic, oil and chilli

400 g spaghetti
4 tablespoons olive oil
4 cloves of garlic
1 peperoncino, *whole or crushed in a mortar*
1 tablespoon chopped parsley
40 g grated pecorino

Bring salt water to the boil, put the spaghetti in and cook till al dente. *Heat some oil and fry the chopped garlic and the crumbled* peperoncino *in it until the garlic is golden yellow. Mix the drained spaghetti with the chopped parsley and the boiling hot oil sauce, and sprinkle the grated pecorino over it. This dish tastes very good even without the parsley, and many people from the Abruzzi also omit the cheese. Some gourmets fish the garlic and the* peperoncino *out of the pan, as far as possible, and enjoy the spaghetti with the hot oil alone, which combines the flavour of the garlic with the heat of the* peperoncino.

The truly purist version of this recipe has an even more delectable flavour. Pour high quality olive oil on to a warmed plate, add pressed garlic juice and crushed peperoncino, *and mix this uncooked sauce with the hot pasta.*

Our favourite dish in Roccaraso, though, was *spaghetti alla puttanesca*, whores' spaghetti; I thought it was an invention of our regular trattoria until I later came across it again in Naples and discovered that it was a speciality from the island of Ischia. The rich and yet light sauce contains black olives, capers, anchovies, tomatoes, garlic and *peperoncino*.

Spaghetti alla puttanesca
'Whores' spaghetti'

400 g spaghetti
500 g tomatoes (or 1 tin peeled tomatoes)
100 ml olive oil
150 g black olives
100 g anchovies preserved in salt
50 g capers preserved in salt
1 clove of garlic
1 peperoncino
salt

First put the spaghetti in salted boiling water. Then bone the anchovies, rinse off the salt under running water, and place in a heavy saucepan. Fry gently until the garlic is golden yellow and the anchovies have disintegrated in the oil. Finally, add the skinned tomatoes, the stoned olives and capers, thoroughly washed and squeezed out, and leave to simmer until the spaghetti is al dente. *Then drain and mix with the sauce.*

The dry herb brandy the landlord always used to offer us at the end of the meal goes very well with the aromatic heat of the cuisine of the Abruzzi. It is called *centerbe* – 'a hundred herbs' – and is distilled from mountain herbs. It is greenish in colour, and so strong that it burns your throat almost as much as a *peperoncino*. The locals maintain that the fire in the glass and the fire on the plate help them survive the cold winter – the fire in the grate is not enough.

I always used to bring a bunch of little fresh pepper pods back home with me from Italy, but now you can buy them in the autumn here too at Italian grocers. After allowing them to dry, crush them in a mortar and you will always have the fiery heat of this wholly natural product to hand; it tastes far better than ground cayenne pepper. I learned this piece of kitchen lore in a Roman *erboristeria*, as the herb and spice shops are called in Italy. They are gradually disappearing, and look like old-fashioned chemists with their earthenware vessels, balances and mortars. The owner, a herb expert, explained to me that powdered herbs are no good because they lose their flavour far too quickly, quite apart from the fact that milling is detrimental to all natural flavours. Peppercorns, too, only maintain their full flavour if they are pounded up in a mortar. The McCormick company, who sell good quality crushed red chillies in glass jars, has clearly realized this too.

Above all though, one spice from the Abruzzi that is renowned throughout Italy is to be found in the Roman *erboristerias* – saffron, which is grown in open fields in the province of L'Aquila. It consists of the reddish-brown stamens of the saffron crocus, which local women separate one by one from their flowers with a needle. To produce one pound of saffron, approximately 75,000 to 150,000 flowers are required.

It's hardly surprising it's so expensive. Today it is sold in little jars containing one gramme. This is enough to season at least ten risottos for four people. The saffron threads used to be pulverized in a mortar, but today Italian housewives prefer to just stir them in hot stock, because if the red threads can be seen in the yellow risotto this shows that real saffron was used rather than a chemical powder.

I subsequently found out how pasta too can be cooked with a saffron sauce in the 'Ristorante Abruzzi' in Rome, near the Fontana di Trevi. *Vermicelli in salsa abruzzese* is a monochrome dish with chopped yellow pumpkin flowers in it as well as saffron.

Vermicelli in salsa abruzzese
Spaghetti from the Abruzzi

400 g spaghetti
1 onion
6–8 pumpkin or marrow flowers
a little stock
olive oil
1 pinch saffron
1 fresh egg
grated pecorino
salt and black pepper

Chop the onion together with the thoroughly washed marrow flowers. Heat some oil in a pan, add the onions and flowers and the saffron, dissolved in a little water; season. Mix well and cook, stirring frequently. After ten minutes, put through a sieve and return to the same pan; thin with some stock and allow to simmer gently for a few minutes. Now remove the sauce from

the heat and combine it with the yolk of an egg and a few
spoonsful of grated pecorino. Mix the spaghetti, boiled in salted
water till al dente, with the hot sauce.

The Abruzzi region is very similar to Sardinia. In this mountainous country, keeping sheep is one of the most important economic activities, and the cuisine is heavily influenced by the habits of the shepherds; pecorino, the ewes' milk cheese, predominates, and lambs and sucking pigs are roasted at open fires. A stew of lamb or mutton is a common accompaniment to pasta. I owe the following recipe to the owner of the 'Ristorante da Nino' near the Piazza del Popolo in Rome.

Tagliatelle con spezzatino d'agnello
Tagliatelle with lamb sauce and peperoni

400 g tagliatelle, salted water
200 g stewing lamb
2 peperoni *(hot peppers)*
2 tomatoes
2 cloves of garlic
2 bay leaves
½ glass white wine
5 tablespoons olive oil
salt and pepper

Slice the lamb into thin strips and season. Heat the olive oil and the garlic and bay leaves in a pan, then add the lamb and brown gently. After fifteen minutes add the white wine; once it has evaporated, add the quartered tomatoes and the sliced peperoni. *Leave the sauce to simmer on very low heat for two*

hours. It may be necessary to add a little water or stock. Season
at the end of cooking. Boil the pasta till al dente, *drain, and*
pour the sauce over it.

It is possible to get to know the cuisine of the Abruzzi at first hand in Rome, as the mountain province is a region of emigration, and the cooks and waiters in many of the best little trattorias in Rome come from there. At Nino's there is almost always an excellent chocolate cake for dessert; you can tell it is home made from the dark chocolate pieces sprinkled over it, which show that the chocolate was grated by hand. I am not completely sure if this is a speciality of the Abruzzi, as the owner of Nino's maintains, but one thing is certain – the cake tastes wonderful and is very easy to make. The original recipe does not include any baking powder, but I have added it, because I think the cake is even better if it is allowed to rise a little.

Torta di cioccolato
Chocolate cake

250 g butter
250 g sugar
5 eggs
250 g ground almonds
150 g grated bitter chocolate
75 g flour
½ packet baking powder
butter and flour for the tin

Cream the butter and sugar and add the whole eggs one by
one, stirring constantly. Then fold in spoonfuls of the

almonds and the chocolate, as well as the flour and the
baking powder. Grease a springform with butter and flour it.
Then add the mixture and bake the cake on low heat for
60–75 minutes till done. It may be sprinkled with icing sugar.

In the 'Abruzzi', the owner hands round glasses of Strega liqueur, which owes its golden yellow colour and pleasantly medicinal flavour to saffron, at the end of the meal, not the spicy centerbe brandy, let alone the sickly sweet Sambuca which is generally *de rigueur* in Rome, served with a coffee bean in the glass.

Naples, tomatoes and mozzarella

Naples was the first Italian city where I lived and worked. After finishing my studies in Zurich, a scholarship from the Italian government took me to Naples. It was in November, and I will never forget the impression the city made on me with its myriad colours, scents, and noises. I was entering a world where the memory of the grey Swiss November soon faded away. Here everything was colourful and bright, here life was played out on the streets even in winter – lemonade stalls decorated with vibrant yellow lemons invited you to drink, and steaming pizzas or crispy fried pumpkin flowers were on offer at every corner. The babble of voices, the honking of horns, the chaotic, nervous life of the narrow streets was like a drug. The coffee was a drug too – in no other Italian city do people make it so strong and tasty. The best coffee was to be had in a little bar in an alley of the glass-covered Galleria, a few drops of coffee essence, thick, foamy and indescribable. It is not just because the Neapolitans are so sociable that people in Naples live on the streets even in winter, but also because there is little or no heating in most houses. I have never felt so cold in my life as I did during that sunny winter in Naples. I lived in a building with no heating at all, and in my room there was just a joke of an electric stove with a tiny ring. It was impossible to read or write at the desk, so I spent many afternoons and evenings in bed under a pile of woollen blankets and – the tip of my nose frozen – read all the Italian authors I didn't know, before Nievo and Svevo, Calvino and Gada, Ungaretti and Montale.

Those of us on scholarship didn't have much money, and so our everyday staple was *spaghetti alla napoletana*, which is excellent even in the cheapest trattorias, cooked *al dente* and with a sauce the secret of which lies in its simplicity, and also of course in the high quality of the local tomatoes, which are sold ripe and sweet at the markets. Edoardo's mother showed my how very quick this dish is to cook. It is made with homemade tomato sauce or with blanched and peeled fresh tomatoes.

Spaghetti alla napoletana
Spaghetti with tomato sauce

400 g spaghetti
1 kg ripe tomatoes, peeled and cut up into small pieces
5 tablespoons olive oil
fresh basil
salt and pepper
50 g grated Parmesan

Put the salted water on to boil for the pasta before starting to make the sauce. Warm the oil, add the tomatoes, season and bring to the boil for a few minutes. When the spaghetti is al dente, *the sauce will be done too. Add the coarsely chopped basil and mix the sauce with the drained spaghetti and the grated Parmesan. Thanks to the short cooking time, the flavour and the beautiful colour of the fresh tomatoes are preserved.*

In the warm summer months, the tomatoes are often not cooked at all, because then they are so ripe and sweet that there would be no point in altering them by cooking. Cut the peeled tomatoes up very small, drain in a sieve and stir in the salt, pepper, olive oil and the finely chopped basil. A drop of pressed

garlic juice may also be added. In a warmed bowl, combine the
hot drained spaghetti with the raw tomato sauce, which has an
exquisite fresh flavour.

The cooking of Naples includes a wealth of fast dishes that accommodate the need of the locals to enjoy a warm snack at all hours of the day and night. This is true both of the street traders with their freshly fried fish, seafood, artichokes and pumpkin flowers, and also of the pizzerias, where pizza is baked without a break from ten o'clock in the morning till two a.m. Here, pizza is a light snack rather than a meal in itself; it consists of a paper-thin and totally crispy dough base, and the classic toppings are tomatoes, mozzarella and fresh basil leaves. The same happy combination also occurs in a variant of spaghetti alla napoletana where the tomatoes are cooked with 100 g mozzarella to make a creamy sauce.

Tomatoes and mozzarella are also the ingredients of an incredible aubergine gratin with the somewhat confusing name of *melanzane alla parmigiana*, or aubergines in the style of Parma. In fact it is only the cheese that comes from Parma; it is grated over the gratin dish before it goes in the oven to enable a fine golden brown crust to form. I first ate this dish with Edoardo's mother as the first course of a Neapolitan Sunday lunch, which usually begins at three and lasts till around nine o'clock at night. You sit with friends and relations in the kitchen, finding time between courses to watch the football on television and discuss it at length, to pop out to the kiosk to buy cigarettes, and to play with the children. This recipe comes from Edoardo's mother too; it calls for quite a lot of time and effort, but it is well worth it.

Melanzane alla parmigiana
Aubergine gratin

4 medium aubergines
salt
1–2 tablespoons flour
olive oil
1 tin peeled tomatoes
fresh basil
2 packets of 150 g of mozzarella
50 g grated Parmesan

Peel the aubergines and cut lengthwise into thin slices; salt and lay between two plates, then put a heavy weight on top so that the bitter juice comes out. This will take about half an hour. Meanwhile, make a mild, fat-free tomato sauce with the tomatoes, the basil and a little salt; it should be boiled for no more than ten minutes. Cut the mozzarella into slices. Next comes the careful frying of the aubergines, which is most of the work. After drying them well with kitchen paper, turn them in the flour, shaking it off well, and fry them in the hot olive oil until they are golden brown on both sides. Wipe off the fat with kitchen paper and put them in a buttered gratin dish in layers with cheese and tomato sauce. After the final layer of aubergines the order of the layers (aubergines – cheese – tomato sauce) is reversed, covering the aubergine first with tomato sauce and finishing with a topping of grated Parmesan. Bake the aubergines in a medium oven for 45–60 minutes. If the crust gets too dark, cover with aluminium foil.

In Italy, this dish is often served as a starter or to accompany

meat. Personally, I think it makes one of the best summer meals
I know with a mixed salad.

Like Vesuvius and the sea, fresh white mozzarella is part of Naples. It is made from the milk of buffalo cows, the so-called *bufale*, and its popularity is not just due to the ease with which it melts on pizzas and other dishes; it is a healthy low-calorie fresh cheese that can be combined with a huge variety of flavours thanks to its delicate milky flavour. Among salads, too, the combination of tomatoes and mozzarella remains a classic. Known as *insalata caprese*, it is one of the archetypal summer dishes that people like to eat even when the heat has almost robbed them of their appetite.

Insalata caprese
Mozzarella and tomato salad

2 packets of 200 g mozzarella
6 ripe tomatoes
salt and pepper
oregano or fresh basil
6 tablespoons olive oil

Slice the mozzarella and the tomatoes. Arrange alternating slices of tomato and cheese on a platter in a tile pattern, sprinkle with salt, pepper and oregano and pour the olive oil over the top. This salad also tastes wonderful if finely-chopped basil leaves are used instead of the oregano. If liked, a few drops of vinegar may be added to the salad, preferably mild red wine vinegar.

To preserve the fresh, milky taste of mozzarella fully, after it is made it is placed in a slightly salted liquid. In Italy you buy it in open glass jars, but for export the little white spheres are individually packed in watertight foil; when opened this should contain a little liquid. If not the mozzarella is no longer fresh.

Mozzarella in carozza – 'mozzarella in a carriage' – is another famous dish, a cheese sandwich fried in oil; it is one of the revelations of the popular cuisine of Naples.

Mozzarella in carozza
Fried cheese sandwich

8 slices bread for toasting
4 thick slices mozzarella
2 eggs
salt
2 tablespoons milk
2 tablespoons flour
olive oil for frying

Remove the crusts from the bread, place one slice of cheese each on four of the slices and cover them with the other four. Dip the edges of the bread briefly in cold water so that they can be pressed tightly closed over the cheese. Beat the eggs with salt and milk until they begin to become foamy. Pour the flour out on to a plate and gently turn the bread round in it on both sides. Heat up plenty of oil in a pan. After turning the sandwiches several times in the egg mixture, fry till golden yellow in the oil. Lift them out with a slotted spoon, allow to drain briefly on kitchen paper, and serve as hot as possible. On menus, mozzarella in carozza *generally figures as a starter, but I find it is a dish that is better suited for a light supper, together with a salad.*

Sometimes I was invited to eat with Piero Gruber. He lived with his parents in a villa on the hill of Capodimonte, from which there is a good view of the city and the sea. The food was served by a butler with white gloves, and a *marchese* from among their neighbours was often invited. It was here that I was introduced one Friday afternoon to the traditional *baccalà alla napoletana*; the sweet and salty sauce contains all the ingredients of the country cooking of Campania.

Baccalà alla napoletana
Neapolitan salt cod

800 g soaked salt cod
1 pound tomatoes
150 g black olives
50 g each of pine kernels and sultanas
1 tablespoon of capers
flour
2 cloves of garlic
olive oil
salt and pepper

Heat the olive oil and the peeled garlic in a saucepan, remove the garlic as soon as it has turned yellow and add the peeled tomatoes, the stoned and chopped olives, the chopped capers, the pine kernels and the soaked and drained sultanas and season. Add 100–200 ml water, stir and allow to simmer for about

twenty minutes on very low heat. Rinse the cod in cold water,
pull off the skin, bone it carefully and cut into fairly large square
pieces. Dry well, turn in the flour and fry in hot oil on both
sides. Remove with a slotted spoon, leave to drain on kitchen
paper and place in a flat ovenproof dish. Pour the sauce on top,
covering the fish well. Bake in a preheated 180° C oven for half
an hour.

This fish dish tasted marvellous, but I couldn't quite understand why on earth people should eat dried fish on Fridays in a maritime city like Naples rather than fresh fish. The Marchese said it was a Catholic tradition; people had eaten salted fish on fast days for centuries throughout Italy from Venice to Palermo, whether it was salt or dried cod, herring or anchovies. The same was true of Spain, Portugal and France. Piero suggested there were practical reasons for this; before the advent of refrigeration, salting was the only way of preserving fish so that it could be transported and sold.

Later, when I discovered *baccalà* cooked in a variety of ways in Rome and Venice, in Ticino and in the south of France, I remembered this conversation, which did not even consider the culinary quality of salt cod. But the powerful, hearty flavour of salted fish, which undergoes a fermentation process during salting, is certainly the most important reason that salt and dried cod are still sold and cooked today at all. Frozen would be cheaper and simpler. But just as people continue to eat dried meat and ham even though they can buy fresh meat from the butcher whenever they wish, there will continue to be a demand for the flavour of salt cod, salted herring and dried beans.

Calabria,
or Cosentino's kitchen

I have never been to Calabria; I owe my knowledge of Calabrian cuisine to Domenico Cosentino, who comes from Catanzaro and learned how to clean mussels and scale and clean fish at the 'Ristorante Carmelina' while he was still at middle school. Since then he has expanded his culinary expertise in theory and practice, making a name for himself as a television chef, cookery writer and journalist, even though his main job is working for an international patent office. Not only does he have an intimate knowledge of regional Italian cookery, he is also up on the latest culinary trends and knows how to adapt traditional dishes to the modern preference for light and delicate food. Naturally he also thinks it is important for cookery to pay attention to the seasons, and so one January he invited me to a meal devoted to Calabrian winter dishes. We were immediately amazed by the many antipasti already waiting for us in brown glazed earthenware dishes: warm fried meatballs, a spicy aubergine purée, three different kinds of olives, bright green broccoli dressed with olive oil and lemon juice, red and yellow peperoni strips seasoned with garlic, olive oil and basil, salted anchovies with red pepper, and a little gratin dish of fresh anchovies arranged in star shapes that the cook took out of the oven just after we arrived. Would we like a *frittata calabrese* as well? We said we would, and Cosentino let us watch him make the omelette; it tastes just as good hot, warm or cold.

Frittata calabrese
Calabrian omelette

3 eggs
freshly grated pecorino
ricotta
unsmoked spicy pork sausage
mint leaves
olive oil
salt and pepper

Beat the eggs, salt, and pepper with a fork, add the pecorino and then the ricotta, cut into small pieces, the crumbled sausage and the torn up mint leaves. Heat the oil in a frying pan and add the egg mixture, shaking the pan as it fries. Then slide on to a lid or a plate and turn it over to fry on the other side as well. The omelette should be set in the middle, but still damp, and a good brown colour on the outside. Cut into pieces like a cake.

The simple country cooking of Calabria is based entirely on the quality of its ingredients. According to Cosentino, you cannot make a *frittata calabrese* without fresh ricotta; the factory-produced ricotta that can be bought today both in Italy and abroad is no good. Luckily, he discovered an Italian grocer that has fresh ricotta made from local milk. It tastes wonderful, though it does not have the powerful flavour of Calabrian ricotta, which is made from the whey of goats' milk. Cosentino says that country goatherds still eat a soup made of warm whey today, to which a piece of fresh ricotta is added. This is their main meal, eaten with a chunk of home-baked bread.

The fresh spicy sausage is also not easy to find outside Calabria.

Cosentino's source for them, like the durum wheat flour, the bottled tomatoes, the olives, the oil, the salted anchovies, the peperoncino and oregano, is Catanzaro Lido, where he has a house where he goes on holiday with his family. But he admits that sausages similar to the Calabrian ones can be found in Italian and Spanish grocers.

One problem with Cosentino's recipes is the quantities. He thinks there is no point counting the basil leaves, weighing the grated cheese or the parsley, or specifying the exact number of onions, carrots or eggs, which are all different sizes. His cookbooks are not for beginners who want everything to be black and white, but for those with some experience of cooking. This does not cause any problems with simple recipes such as the aubergine purée, spread on bread as a starter or served with boiled fish.

Polpa di melanzane
Aubergine purée

2 aubergines
salt
olive oil
garlic
basil leaves

Cube the aubergines and put them in a gratin dish; season with oil and salt and place in a medium oven. Cook for about twenty minutes till done, turning occasionally. With a fork, crush them to make a purée; this takes quite some strength and persistence. The aubergines should definitely not be peeled, as the skin is responsible for the strong, slightly bitter flavour of the purée. To finish, mix the aubergines with little slices of garlic, basil leaves cut into strips and olive oil.

> *The flavour of this purée is unique; it could be described as a kind of aubergine essence.*

The regional confusion of Italian fish terminology is almost as striking as with pasta, where – to give just one example – filled square pasta pockets are called ravioli, anolini or agnolotti, depending on the region. The small sea fish that we call sardines or anchovies have a confusing variety of names too; in Italian, they are sarde, sardine, acciughe or alici. In any case, Cosentino was quite sure that for the gratin, braised in the oven and seasoned with oregano, nothing would do apart from the exquisite little fish with the blue-black back that the Calabrians call *alice*.

Alici ariganati
Anchovies with oregano

400 g fresh anchovies
olive oil
3 spoons wine vinegar
salt
oregano

Clean the anchovies under the tap, removing the head, cutting open the gut, cleaning them out and draining thoroughly. Lay them out in a star shape in a gratin dish wiped with oil; sprinkle a little vinegar and oil over them, and season with salt and oregano. Put them in a preheated 200° C oven for ten minutes. They taste best warm rather than hot.

But for me the greatest discovery of this Calabrian meal was the pure, rich flavour of the simple pulses that Cosentino used to make the soup. First we had a *macco di fave*, an ancient dish made from dried *fave*, the original bean variety, broad beans. They played an important nutritional role even in prehistoric times, but in northern and central Europe they were largely replaced by runner beans and used for the most part just as cattle fodder. In Mediterranean countries, though, they remain popular. Before then I had only ever eaten them fresh; in Rome, you often get the juicy green pods as a starter – after removing them from their pods you enjoy the fresh tender half-ripe seeds raw, like nuts, with fresh pecorino and a slice of salami.

Macco di fave
Broad bean soup

200 g dried fave (broad beans)
1 large onion
2 peeled tinned tomatoes
olive oil, salt

Soak the beans overnight in cold water. The following morning, peel the skin off them, rinse and put in a saucepan with a litre of cold water and the chopped onion. Boil for an hour and a half before adding the tomatoes and 4 tablespoons of oil; leave to boil for another hour. Then season the soup and serve with grated pecorino, crushed peperoncino *and a little fresh olive oil if liked.*

While eating this tasty soup, which the tomatoes make a beautiful red colour, I realized that north of the Alps, there is a tendency to over-season bean, lentil and pea dishes, especially by cooking them with smoked bacon, with the result that their characteristic flavour is obscured. Cosentino also pointed out that the country cooking of his native province depends on the proper combination of just a few fundamental elements. Even dishes completely different in character have the same ingredients, olive oil, tomatoes, onions, garlic, mint, basil, *peperoncino* and pecorino. Stock cubes and tins are useless in this cuisine, which is entirely dependent on the powerful flavour of natural produce that is available all year round.

A second example of Calabrian winter cooking was a soup made of white beans and the slightly bitter dark green *catalogna*, for which native wild chicory may be substituted north of the Alps.

Minestra di fagioli con catalogna
Bean soup with catalogna

200 g white beans
1 stick celery
500 g catalogna
olive oil
2 cloves of garlic

Soak the beans overnight in cold water; the next day, rinse them and put in a saucepan with the celery and a litre of water, and allow to boil for one hour. Trim and wash the catalogna and boil in salt water till done. Then heat olive oil in a heavy pan, gently fry the peeled garlic and add the vegetables, followed by the beans and some water; reduce for ten to fifteen minutes, until the soup has the right slightly creamy consistency. Season and serve with grated pecorino.

In Calabria, people will say of someone who is doing well, 'He eats pork and homemade pasta.' For centuries, the pig was a Calabrian peasant's greatest asset; even in areas where olives grow, pork fat is often used for cooking, and pig's blood is still used today to make the traditional sanguinaccio, a sweet black pudding whose ingredients include milk, sugar, cocoa, almonds and mint. We tried some at Cosentino's, but it did taste slightly rancid.

In southern Italy eggs are not used to make home-made pasta, just water and flour. This is not the flour sold in this country, but durum wheat flour produced in Apulia and Sicily, with an especially high protein content. This means it contains more gluten, which is what makes pasta firm. Cosentino showed us how the housewives of Catanzaro make their *maccaroni di casa*: they wrap a small piece of dough round a stick mould and roll it to an even thinness by hand. The hardest step is then pulling the stick out so as to leave intact the hole where the flavoursome pasta sauce will go.

For dessert a large basket of fresh and dried fruit was brought to the table, including pomegranates, oranges, mandarins, nuts and roast chestnuts – they taste surprisingly good cold. There was also red fennel in a bowl of cold water and in a second bowl were salted lupin seeds. After this light and soothing interlude, recalling the antipasto with its raw, salty ingredients, the final act was coffee and cannoli, crispy pastry rolls filled with sweetened ricotta and candied fruits that once again did Cosentino's kitchen full credit.

Sicily, the land where the orange trees bloom

If you want to experience an orange grove in its full glory, you have to go to Sicily in November to see the orange plantations on the slopes of Mount Etna near Catania. In November the reddish-yellow fruits begin to ripen in the dark foliage; the sky is transparently clear and blue, and the air is as mild as a northern September. It is no accident that the Sicilians call their orange groves *giardini d'arancio* – orange gardens – for they are far from being extensive plantations. The area between the sea and the slopes of Mount Etna is narrow, and it has been lovingly cared for and irrigated. One expert told me that it is the sun that makes Sicilian oranges so sweet, but the shining red colour of the peel and the flesh is due to the cold nights. In tropical countries there are only green oranges. But even for blood oranges, too much cold can be dangerous. If the temperature falls below two degrees, the siren-like screaming of the *ventole* starts up in the plantations – these wind machines are motor-driven propellers that stir up the air at a height of about fifteen metres so the frost cannot descend to the level of the orange trees. The juicy blood oranges harvested here really do have a flavour like no other oranges in the world.

It was thanks to a lucky accident, or rather a chain of lucky accidents, that years ago I got to know the landscape of these gardens, with all their black walls made of pumice and the snow-topped peak of Mount Etna in the background. At the time I was working on a paper and I had got so involved in my work that I had kept putting off my holidays, and now all of a sudden it was November. I thought that in this grey season I was most likely to find some remnants of sun and warmth in Sicily, and I bought myself a plane ticket to Catania. I would see what the weather was like once I had arrived before deciding whether to have a sightseeing holiday or go to the beach. When I came out of the airport terminal to look around for a taxi, my eye was caught by an empty bus, which said it was going to Taormina. Without thinking about it very much, I got in and drove along the coast road at dusk; I was the only passenger. In Taormina I asked about a room in a hotel on the main road, not realizing I had already reached my holiday destination. The next morning I discovered I was the only guest in the hotel, and the wife of the manager invited me to take my meals with the family in the large kitchen. In so doing, she made the decision for me about what to do with my holiday, which had still been uncertain. As well as getting to know one Sicilian family in my hosts, including two thirteen-year-old (twin) brothers, a daughter of eighteen, an unmarried sister and a grandmother, I was also invited to visit their friends and relations around and about Taormina; in this way I discovered the whole eastern coast, above all the citrus gardens on Mount Etna, which belonged to the family.

Much to my surprise, when the first oranges were ripe, an orange salad was served to accompany the meatballs – which are a very popular dish in Sicily, because the meat of cattle slaughtered locally tends to be pretty tough. This orange salad was dressed with vinegar and oil and garnished with black olives. It has a wonderfully exotic flavour, and I later incorporated it into my culinary repertoire as a starter.

Insalata di arance piccante
Spicy orange salad

4 medium oranges, not too sweet
10 black olives
100 g ricotta or mozzarella
1 teaspoon olive oil
salt and pepper

Peel the oranges carefully, cut them in half and then slice thinly.
Stone and halve the olives. Cut up the cheese into small pieces.
Then combine these ingredients with the dressing and leave to
sit for half an hour before serving.

Just as tasty, indeed maybe even more special, is the lemon salad. By this I mean slices of lemon dressed with a normal vinaigrette. Though that may sound strange, it has to be tried at least once. I ate this salad too for the first time in the 'Hotel Victoria' in Taormina, and even with the rather unripe lemons we are able to buy here I think it is splendid. The lemon juice will not tolerate the addition of other ingredients, except perhaps a bit of mustard in the dressing.

The importance of oranges for the Sicilians can also be seen from the fact that the most characteristic dish of the island takes both its name and its shape from them; I mean *arancini di riso*. These are filled rice balls the size of small oranges, fried golden yellow in hot oil – a speciality that can be found in the smallest village, in every bar or trattoria. For me, they are the quintessence of Sicilian cookery, a simple, rustic and yet also imaginative and sophisticated dish that could only have been invented on this poor island with its colourful history and its mixed population descended from Greeks, Normans, Arabs, Spaniards and Frenchmen. A comparison with *supplì*, the Roman version of this dish, makes it clear why; these are little balls of rice filled with a piece of Provolone cheese and deep fried, producing threads when you bite into them. The filling of *arancine*, on the other hand, is much richer and more delicate. It consists of a fine meat stew mixed with vegetables, cheese or hard-boiled egg, depending on the area. In other words, these crispy little balls contain a tiny meal. They may be eaten hot, warm or cold, and it is always easy to make them hot and crispy again in the oven. Whether as a starter, a main course or a snack, they always taste far superior to any sandwich.

I also found out all sorts of things about Sicilian wine from my hotel family in Taormina. Don Nicola, the hotelier's cousin, owned a small vineyard on Mount Etna, and he told me that orange cultivation was increasingly pushing out wine-making, which was less profitable, even though the Etna wine is one of the finest growths of the whole of Sicily. I was able to confirm this, as our table wine came from Don Nicola's cellar; he complained bitterly that the quality of Sicilian wines was not recognized in Europe, maintaining that it is incomparably higher than that of other Italian wines, including Chianti and Barolo. Yet only Marsala was exported from Sicily, he went on, and that is really no more than a good mass-produced wine, more appropriate for cooking than for drinking. To show me the difference between mass produced stuff and the genuine article, he uncorked a fifteen-year-old bottle of Marsala; it was hardly sweet at all, the colour of pale gold, and had a rich delicate flavour.

Sicilians often use Marsala to cook with, and it adds a pleasant and slightly exotic note to many dishes. One of the best known of them is *scaloppine al marsala*; it is also very popular in the rest of Italy. In meat-poor Sicily it is always made with pork escalopes, not veal.

Scoloppine al marsala
Pork escalopes (loin end)

flour
salt and pepper
80 g butter
1 small glass Marsala

*Season the flour with salt and pepper and turn the escalopes in
it. Fry them on both sides in 50 g butter, then add the Marsala;
reduce, then add a little water and the remaining butter. Pour
the sauce over the escalopes and serve.*

The best recipe I took home with me from Taormina was for *carote alla
marsala*, namely carrots stewed with butter and a glass of Marsala rather
than being boiled in salted water, as we normally do.

Carote alla marsala
Carrots with Marsala

800 g carrots
50 g butter
½ glass Marsala
salt and pepper

*Clean the carrots and slice them. Melt the butter and very
gently fry the sliced carrot in it. Then add the Marsala and the*

salt and pepper and allow to stew on very low heat, covered, for
15–30 minutes till done. Shake the pan occasionally so they do
not stick. You may need to add a little extra water or stock.

The chief food of the Sicilians is of course fish, which is available in the three seas by which the island is surrounded – the Ionian Sea, the Tyrrhenian Sea and the Mediterranean. Tuna and swordfish are the favourites, but – as on all Italian coasts – sardines are the commonest. The *sarde a beccafico* that we ate in a trattoria in Catania show how this cheap fish can be transformed into a decorative and subtle dish.

Beccafico means 'warbler', and the name of the dish thus means 'sardines like birds'. I only understood the meaning of this when I saw the great platter on which the fish, headless, stuffed, rolled and fried a crispy brown, lay garnished with bay leaves. You could have taken them for stuffed thrushes. This recipe is known throughout Sicily, and every province has its own version.

Sarde a beccafico
Stuffed sardines

1 kg fresh sardines
salt and pepper
50 g raisins
100 g breadcrumbs
200 ml olive oil
4 tablespoons pine kernels
1 tablespoon chopped parsley
4 anchovy fillets
50 g pecorino
bay leaves, juice of one lemon

Wash the sardines, remove the heads, cut open at the belly, and gut them. Carefully remove the main bones so that the sardines remain intact and may be opened up. Wash again and dry well with kitchen paper. Sprinkle with salt. Soak the raisins in a little lukewarm water. Brown 40 g breadcrumbs in some olive oil, place in a bowl and mix with the drained and dried raisins, the pine kernels, the parsley, the finely chopped anchovy fillets, some tiny pieces of cheese, and salt and pepper. Work all this into a paste with a wooden spoon. Place a spoonful of filling on top of each sardine before rolling up so that the tail is on top; hold together with a toothpick. Put the sardines in a gratin dish, placing between each roll a bay leaf, drizzle with lemon juice and oil and bake for 30–40 minutes in a medium oven. They also taste delicious warm or cold as a starter.

When people mention the rest of Italy in Sicily, they talk about the 'continent', showing the proud confidence of an island people with its own history, its own culture and its own cuisine – and its own baking tradition too, which probably developed under Arab influence in the early middle ages. Sicily is an Eldorado for all who love sweet goodies; everything is sweeter here than elsewhere, the pies and cakes, the sweets and the ice cream. In addition, the basic raw ingredients – honey, almonds and pistachios – grow on the island. Rorrone is made from them as well, cooked according to an old monastic recipe on a very low heat for twelve hours. Another monastic speciality made of almonds and sugar are the *frutti della Martorana*, marzipan fruits from the Martorana monastery in Palermo painted the colour of plants that are incredibly realistic; there are blemished apples, rotting pears, mouldy oranges, and figs eaten by insects, all small, delicate and completely true to life. They are also sold in the best cake shops of Catania and Messina.

Among the simple desserts that are also made by Sicilian housewives is *cassata*, which in Sicily does not mean ice cream; it is a sponge base filled with ricotta and a colourful bouquet of candied fruit.

Cassata alla siciliana
Sicilian ricotta cake

1 round unfilled sponge cake
750 g ricotta
400 g icing sugar
1 pinch of cinnamon
500 g mixed candied fruit
1 bar bitter chocolate
2 glasses Maraschino

Mix the ricotta up with the icing sugar and put in the fridge overnight. Put the most attractive fruit, about half, to one side to use as a garnish. Coarsely chop the remaining fruit and crumble the chocolate into small pieces; cut the sponge in half to make two rounds and soak them both in Maraschino. Mix the cinnamon into the ricotta and beat with a wooden spoon until smooth and creamy. Reserving 4 tablespoons of this sauce, combine the rest with the chopped fruit and chocolate. Line a springform evenly with greaseproof paper or aluminium foil and place one half of the sponge on the bottom; spread it with half of the sauce, put the second sponge round on top and fill with the remaining ricotta mixture. Place the side of the springform around the cake and refrigerate for at least six hours. Before eating, invert the cake onto a platter, spread the reserved sauce over the top and garnish with the candied fruit. The cassata should be eaten as cold as possible.

The silver-green artichoke fields of Sardinia

It is well known that the low season is the most pleasant time to travel in Italy. Visiting Taormina in November, Venice in December and Naples in March is now the only way to see these tourist destinations properly. But Sardinia in January is the best of all. I went with Irene because neither of us had any enthusiasm for snowbound landscapes; we longed for the mild sea breeze of the south. We couldn't have made a better choice!

We suspected as much as we were coming in to land at Alghero airport and could see the shining green country beneath us, disappearing off to towards the blue-grey sea in a succession of beautifully curved bays and foothills. As we stepped from the plane a fresh, salty sea wind was blowing, and it was not to leave us for the rest of our time in Sardinia.

On the bus trip to Alghero, we saw silver olive groves, dark green holm oaks, rows of cypresses planted as a windbreak for brown fields, and plenty of grazing land peppered with grey rocks that were easily confused with the whitish dots of the sheep herds. We had not reserved a hotel in Alghero, as we wanted to make discoveries and stay where we felt like rather than planning our holiday in advance. All we knew about Alghero was the name of a restaurant, 'I Tugheri', which means 'peasant's hovel'. We found it in an alley in the old town, and when we walked into the little room we realized at once that this was a good place. A fire glowed in the chimney, and the simple wooden tables were reminiscent of a Spanish taverna. We asked what Sardinian specialities they had, and for the first course we got a plate of *malloredus* – delicately-shaped pasta that are also called *gnochetti*. They are practically the Sardinian national dish, and we often ate them again. Irene observed that these compact little mouthfuls are just as apt a reflection of the unsentimental character of the Sardinians as the long, curling spaghetti are of the expansive nature of the mainland Italians.

We never had authentic homemade *malloredus*, dyed yellow with saffron, during our entire stay on the island, even though homemade fare generally predominates in Sardinian cooking; in this respect, the local pasta industry has clearly got its own way. The Sardinians prefer to eat their pasta in tomato sauce enriched with Sardinian sausage. A woman from Alghero whom I later met in the hotel told me the secret of this recipe. As we cannot obtain Sardinian sausages, Spanish chorizos or south Italian sausages (but not ones with too much pepper) may be used.

Sugo di pomodoro con salsiccia
Tomato sauce with sausage

3 tablespoons of olive oil
half an onion
parsley
200 g fresh pork sausage
1 tin peeled tomatoes

Slowly fry the finely chopped onion and parsley in the oil until soft before adding the skinned sausages, cut into small pieces; allow to take colour, stirring occasionally, before adding the tomatoes. Leave the sauce to simmer very gently for 15–20 minutes and add to the pasta with some freshly grated pecorino sardo.

This tomato sauce with sausage is one of the simple culinary discoveries you generally only make in areas where the cooking remains as straightforward and natural as it is in Sicily. In addition, the pecorino sardo, the hard Sardinian sheep's cheese, used for grating, has a quite extraordinarily rich, fine flavour, so that every dish where it is used instead of Parmesan acquires a new and somehow rustic charm. It's worth a try, and this pecorino can be found in any Italian delicatessen. We quickly felt at our ease in Alghero, which may have something to do with the fact that this little fishing town has a Catalonian rather than a Sardinian feel – it was founded by Catalans in the 14th century. The great watchtowers and walls recall this period, and the inhabitants still speak Catalan to this day. The town's Iberian origin can be seen even in the oldest section, huddled together on a little promontory, with its gothically decorated alleys and the cheery atmosphere of its cafés and bars. We found the hotel 'La Tronas' on the other side of the seafront from the town – it sticks out into the breakers almost like an island, so the music of wind and waves is in one's ears day and night. It was just what we were looking for.

The next day we went exploring; we drove a hire car from the coast to the interior. Our destination was the most famous Romanesque church on the island, the *Santissima Trinità di Saccargia*, which stands all on its own among the mountains to the south of Sassari. This raw, uninhabited area feels like mountain country, even though it is only 400 m above sea level, because much of Sardinia consists of a granite massif, with many steep drops, but quite low, where there is only thin pasture and such undemanding plants as agave, cork trees and prickly pears. In the isolation of this rocky landscape the monastic church, built from black basalt and white limestone, seems almost miraculous. It was erected in the 12th century by architects from Pisa in the same style that was fashionable in Tuscany at the time, where it often seems almost too decorative. In the bitter and unforgiving landscape of Sardinia, a severe greatness and purity emanates from these black and white buildings. This is also true of the many other Romanesque churches, which rise up out of forlorn meadows and fields in the northern half of the island.

On the way back to Sassari we had lunch in the single restaurant in the splendid hill village of Ploaghe. It was a bare and rather uninviting establishment, but we thought it must be reliable, as the customers were locals. There was no need to request Sardinian specialities here. First we had a dish of the familiar maloreddus with tomato sauce and sausage, followed by a choice of lamb stew with olives or pork chops. I picked the stew, though it was not made of lamb meat, but offal ranging from the heart to the melts – delicious. Irene had the chop, with artichokes as a side dish. The silver-green artichoke fields we had flown past on our way to Alghero had made her keen to try some. She got a mixture of artichokes and potatoes that did not look all that appetising, but which then turned out to be one of Sardinia's country specialities – not just cheap and nutritious but also utterly delicious. We had the same dish again later in simple country restaurants, and I found the recipe in a book on Sardinian cookery.

Carciofi e patate
Artichokes with potatoes

6 artichokes
6 small potatoes
tomato purée
1 onion
1 bunch parsley
olive oil
1 lemon
salt and pepper

Clean the artichokes, cutting off hard or wilted leaves; halve or quarter them, depending on size, and place in water acidulated with lemon juice. Only the small Italian artichokes may be used

for this recipe – the large French ones are not suitable. Heat up
half a glass of olive oil in a pot and gently fry the finely chopped
onion and parsley in it. Add the tomato purée, having dissolved
it in a little warm water. Leave to cook on very low heat, then
add ¼ litre water and the pealed and diced potatoes and
vegetables. Season.

By the time both the vegetables are soft, the sauce should
have thickened up – if not, turn up the heat a little and allow to
reduce a while longer.

The first time we ate this dish, really almost a meal in itself, we did not know that Sardinian cooking is so elementary, so archaic, that it includes neither vegetables nor salad. Within this tradition, a celebratory meal has always meant pasta with meat, but the everyday meals of the Sardinian shepherds consisted of little more than bread with tomatoes or wild fennel. There are no boiled vegetables, because they are not worth cooking – with the exception of the nutritious combination of potatoes and artichokes. When without thinking I asked for a fennel salad in Ploaghe, I got a plate of roughly-chopped fennel, and the cook did not understand my request for oil, vinegar and salt. Eventually she did bring me a dish of salt and a bottle of oil from the kitchen. The blue-green artichokes of Sardinia, the leaves of which end in a yellow thorn, are the only artichokes that taste just as good raw as cooked. You can pull off the leaves and dip them in a light mayonnaise or in olive oil seasoned with salt and pepper. The fleshy bottoms of the leaves may also be finely chopped, together with the base, and combined with a green salad, lending it a wonderfully earthy and springlike flavour. The long, strong stalks are almost as important as the artichokes themselves, and those in the know pick their artichokes according to the length of the stalk rather than by size. Peel them rather more radically than asparagus to reveal the tender light green marrow; cut it in pieces and add to salad, also raw. These winter artichokes, which disappear from the market during March, taste very good cooked as well as raw.

Carciofi lessi
Boiled artichokes

4 artichokes
salt
olive oil
parsley

Prepare the stalks as described, and cut them up. Remove the outermost hard leaves from the artichokes, cut off the upper two thirds or so and halve or quarter according to size. It is important to prepare the artichokes rigorously, using only the really tender parts. Cook at a rolling boil for ten to fifteen minutes till done, sprinkle with chopped parsley and pour a little good olive oil over them.

These artichokes go well with grilled meat, but they do also make a wonderful vegetable starter.

On a cool rainy morning we took the train to Sassari and immersed ourselves in Sardinian prehistory in the archeological museum. Most of all, we were impressed by the bronze figurines from the 7th and 8th centuries B.C., *bronzetti* as they are called, which depict geometrically stylized yet still very expressive archers and wrestlers, also deer and sheep. For lunch we went to the 'Trattoria Migala' in the Via Turritana, a narrow, lively street running straight through the old town to the cathedral square. The concierge of our hotel had told us the address, and it can be recommended to every visitor to the island who wants to experience something more than the beach and hotel cooking. The long room with its vaulted ceiling leads into the kitchen at the back. This kitchen, which is also where the family lives, is one step higher than the restaurant, so that it seems like a stage. The television was on, and a young man sat on a chair next to it reading the paper and warming his feet at the coal brazier on the floor. Mrs. Migala was busy at the stove turning cheap cuts of lamb into delicacies. Roast lamb is not to be found here, but instead there are little lamb's feet (*piedini d'agnello*) baked with parsley and garlic, lamb tripe seasoned with herbs, wrapped around little skewers and grilled (*sa corda a cordula*). Customers who don't feel like offal can have a hearty lamb stew in tomato sauce, its intense flavour derived from wild mountain fennel. Mrs. Migala, who gave me the recipe, thinks it tastes good with ordinary fennel too.

Spezzatino d'agnello con finocchio
Lamb stew with fennel

800 g cubed lamb
1 onion
3–4 medium fennels
1 tin peeled tomatoes, or 1 pound fresh tomatoes
olive oil, salt

Brown the pieces of lamb well in hot oil, season and add the finely chopped onion once they are a nice golden brown colour; fry gently till the onions turn yellow, then add the tomatoes and leave the stew to cook, covered, for an hour and a half till done. Half an hour before the end, put the quartered fennels in salted water, boil till just done, and combine with the lamb stew before serving. The flavours of fennel and lamb marry well.

But my most vivid impression of Sardinian cuisine was gained not in the flesh, but during a two-hour conversation in a train compartment between

Sassari and Macomer. Irene and I were travelling to Nuoro, and the four young women we got talking to were teachers from Cagliari who had spent the festive period with their families in the north of Sardinia and were now returning to the capital for the new school term. They told us all about the cookery of the island, which is really an increasingly consistent, thrifty and painstaking approach to natural ingredients as it has evolved over two thousand years rather than a culinary tradition in the normal sense. They described the scent of myrtle branches and the characteristic taste it gives to meat roasted over a wood fire; they explained the difference between ordinary fennel and the mountain variety, as well as telling us that Sardinian shepherds have known how to make yoghurt since the beginning of time. (The sheep's milk *gioddu* that we bought a few days later in a shop in Sassari was rather too sour for our taste.) In the midst of this interesting discussion one of the teachers got her suitcase down from the luggage rack and took a tin of traditional Sardinian Christmas biscuits out of it; they delighted us with their beautiful decorative glazes and their dusting of icing sugar and tiny little coloured sugar beads. It seems to me that it is a reflection of the Sardinian character that everything made by hand on the island is especially delicate and shapely, from the little bronze figures in the museum to the malloredus pasta and the aromatic sweet *papassinus* – I wrote down the recipe:

Papassinus
Sardinian Christmas biscuits

500 g flour
150 g sugar
100 g lard or butter
5 g baking powder
2 eggs

300 g sultanas
200 g almonds
100 g shelled walnuts
1 teaspoon aniseed
2–3 cloves
cinnamon, salt
flour and butter
icing sugar

Mix the flour, baking powder, sugar, the unbeaten eggs, and the butter or lard in a bowl and knead the mixture well until it is soft and stretchy. Now combine it with the other ingredients: the grated almonds and walnuts, the sultanas, soaked in warm water, the aniseed and the cloves, crushed in a mortar, a pinch of cinnamon and a little salt. Sprinkle flour on the table, roll the mixture out 1 cm thick, and cut into small diamonds. Put the biscuits on a buttered baking tray and cook in a moderate oven (150° C) for about ten minutes. Remove from the tray immediately and dust with icing sugar.

Index of Recipes